The Greatest Love
Story Ever Told

The Greatest Love Story Ever Told

AN ORAL HISTORY

MEGAN MULLALLY **&** NICK OFFERMAN

DUTTON

DUTTON

An imprint of Penguin Random House LLC
375 Hudson Street
New York, New York 10014

Copyright © 2018 by Megan Mullally and Nick Offerman
Penguin supports copyright. Copyright fuels creativity, encourages diverse
voices, promotes free speech, and creates a vibrant culture. Thank you for
buying an authorized edition of this book and for complying with copyright
laws by not reproducing, scanning, or distributing any part of it in any form
without permission. You are supporting writers and allowing Penguin to
continue to publish books for every reader.

**DUTTON and the D colophon are registered trademarks of
Penguin Random House LLC.**

Chapter opening photographs by Emily Shur
Illustration and lettering by Meryl Rowin

LIBRARY OF CONGRESS CATALOGING-IN-PUBLICATION DATA
has been applied for.

ISBN 9781101986677 (hardcover)
ISBN 9781101986684 (ebook)

Printed in the United States of America
1   3   5   7   9   10   8   6   4   2

While the authors have made every effort to provide accurate telephone numbers,
Internet addresses, and other contact information at the time of publication,
neither the publisher nor the authors assume any responsibility for errors or for
changes that occur after publication. Further, the publisher does not have any
control over and does not assume any responsibility for authors or third-party
websites or their content.

Penguin is committed to publishing works of quality and integrity. In that
spirit, we are proud to offer this book to our readers; however, the story,
the experiences, and the words are the authors' alone.

For Nick

For Megan

CONTENTS

CONTENTS

Blastoff!

Megan: All right! Bum-ba-da-dum! Blastoff! *(Laughs)* This is the introduction to our book. Carefully and meticulously handcrafted, word by word.

Nick: Start your engines.

M: This book consists of our time-tested insights into a number of topics, mostly in the areas of math and science.

N: It's riddled with sordid details.

M: Sordid math details?

N: That's right.

M: Like pi . . .

N: There are specific algorithms we created concerning the relationship between a woman and a man . . .

M: The birds and the bees.

N: The body produces its own lubrication in many instances...

M: Oh, wait a minute. This is the intro! Dude!

N: That's physics!

M: No, no. Too soon! We do get into lubricants of various kinds. But not until later on in the book. Let's not open with that.
So, Nick, how would you describe this kick-ass sheaf?

N: To my way of thinking, it's an illustration of a relationship that the reader might find surprisingly normal. When all you have by which to judge a relationship are some grippingly cute Instagram videos, it might not occur to one that there's a lot of banal real life.

M: So this book is all the boring stuff? *(Laughs)*

N: Yeah.

M: Great! It's going to sell like hotcakes.

N: It's more than just cuteness and puzzles with us. There is also a great deal of tedium.

M: We wanted to make sure we got that down on paper.

N: Yes. We intend to elaborate for your reading pleasure.

M: Who would you say is the ideal audience for this book?

N: Altar boys?

M: *(Laughs)* This is a multigenerational, multigenerational, postmodernist deconstruction of the greatest love story ever told. Meaning, our relationship.

N: It's for readers young and old, male and female, as well as LGBTQ...

M: ...AI.

N: AI. And also every race, religion, every creed, every political leaning will find something to learn about the body's ability to lubricate itself.

M: No! Well, all right...I have to concede, that is what the book is about.

N: When you think about it, what we all have in common is a sort of assemblage of meat that has interesting nooks and crannies.

M: Well, yeah, but then you have to find another meat assemblage with its own nooks and crannies, and then you have to start making the love.

N: You've hooked me. If I were reading this introduction, I would now plunge ahead to chapter one.

M: That's the hook of the book. Meatloaf.

N: Meatloaf...with gravy.

M: Oh god. *(Laughs)* You've circled back around.
So, yes, it is in fact a book about the love affair—the nonplatonic relationship—between Nick Offerman and Megan Mullally, married couple and holders of

social media accounts. That's probably our biggest claim to fame, right?

N: Yes, that's our thing.

M: My whole thing is really just my Twitter.

N: Two people who have thrilled millions upon social media. And also done some other things.

M: And two people who are extremely devoted to athletics. Sports! Sports of all kinds.

N: If you love sports . . .

M: You're going to fucking shit over this book.

N: You're going to blow a load.

M: He's back to the lubricants here.

N: That just proves my point.

M: We have groundbreakingly divided this searing examination of a relationship between two human beings into chapters with different subject matters and headings. It's an oral history presented to you in an organized yet playful fashion, dotted here and there with photography and cute drawings.

N: Before you dive in, make sure you've had a good meal. You'll want to make sure you're hydrated. And if you're of age, a little bit of intoxication would not hurt the consumption of this tome. And then you may want to buckle up. Actually strap into a seat, because otherwise you might end up on the floor. If you're wearing a hat, go ahead and remove it, because it's guaranteed to fly off by the end of chapter three.

M: All right . . . I don't think we've oversold it.

N: No, I don't think that, of the many dangers facing us . . .

M: I think we've exercised a good deal of restraint in our praise of our own book about ourselves.

N: Antony and Cleopatra . . .

M: Fuck off.

N: Samson and Delilah . . .

M: Get lost.

N: Bogart and Bacall . . .

M: Never had a chance.

N: Suck it.

M: All right! See you guys in the book!

N: See you there!

CHAPTER 1

The Story Of How We Met

Megan: Hi, Dad.

Nick: Hi!

M: We're starting our book now. What day is it?

N: Wednesday. It's the eighth. Of February. Two thousand and seventeen.

M: So let's talk about how we met.

N: The year was 2000.

M: That's right. I agree with you so far.

N: The month was April? May? *(Sounds unsure)*

M: *(Firmly)* April. I have the actual date written down at home in my old Filofax.

N: I love the way that you take note of important moments and fare-thee-wells.

M: And here we are, writing a book, so I guess the joke's on ... somebody?

N: Do you think we have enough?

M: *(Laughing)* The End. Actually, I think that we should just list a bunch of dates. That could be the book.

N: And then I could record what I wrote on a Post-it about those dates?

M: It could almost be like a *Farmers' Almanac*.

N: I had been in Los Angeles for a couple of years, and I was having a pretty lousy time with the transition between Chicago theater and a life in Los Angeles.

M: How old were you when you moved to Los Angeles?

N: It was Christmas of 1996, so I was twenty-six.

M: I was twenty-six when I moved to Los Angeles. But we weren't twenty-six at the same time.

N: No. And that won't be the last coincidental set of numbers you'll read about.

M: Not the first, nor the last.

N: Not within these 1,200 pages.

M: A 1,200-page comedy book about relationships.

N: Wait until you get to volume three!
I was depressed, I was drinking a lot. *(Laughing)* Drinking a lot and falling down with regularity.

M: You were basically homeless. You were sleeping on a couch in someone's basement.

N: I had a domicile with a locking door. That's a home.

M: Mmm-hmm...

N: There was a place to hang my hat.

M: Where did you go to the bathroom?

N: This is a comedy book.
I told my friends—all three of them—"Guys, I need to do a play. That's what's going to save me."

M: We met doing a play called *The Berlin Circle* in 2000. How did you get involved in the play?

N: Two of the friends I put the word out to were Nicole Arbusto and Joy Dickson, champion casting directors, who had put me in a movie. They knew me from a Mike Leigh play at the Odyssey Theatre. They also knew of Bart DeLorenzo and the Evidence Room theater company, and they said, "Bart's doing this crazy play and has a part in it for you."

M: I had started my first band, Supreme Music Program, at that point. We had done this crazy performance art show at the Coast Playhouse in West Hollywood.

The guy who coproduced it told me that some people he knew were doing a play downtown and they were hoping I might be in it. I read it, and I thought it was weird but interesting. This was between the second and third seasons of *Will & Grace*, during my four-month hiatus.

N: What was the popularity of *Will & Grace* after two seasons?

M: It was high. It was maybe at orange. It wasn't quite at red alert. Maybe yellowish orange. But obviously I wasn't any kind of a big sensation, since I was free to do an equity waiver play in downtown Los Angeles that nobody had ever heard of.

N: Was there a moment in those first two seasons when it dawned on the collective *Will & Grace* family that "Oh, this is off the hook"?

M: *Will & Grace* started off on Monday nights, and we didn't have an overabundance of viewers. They moved it to Tuesday, and after the first season, they reran the whole season over the summer. Which is something they never do anymore, but it's such a smart move. And all these new viewers found the show. Then they moved it to Thursday, and it became a big deal. But there was some foreshadowing, even when we were doing the pilot. Very early on, one of the big swinging dicks who worked at the network...

N: Debra Messing?

M: *(Laughs)* Hilarious. Don Ohlmeyer, who was working at the network or the studio or something—he was a good friend of O.J.'s, if that tells you anything. The cast was sitting outside on a break while we were shooting the pilot. So we're sitting out there—Debra, Eric, Sean Hayes, and me—and Don Ohlmeyer saunters up to us. This was completely unprecedented in my experience as an actor, and I was thirty-nine at the time and had done a ton of TV pilots. The brass did not fraternize with the chattel. Debra, who smoked at the time, was going to have a cigarette, but she couldn't find a match. Don Ohlmeyer handed her his solid-gold Cartier lighter. She lit her cigarette and went to hand it back, and he said, "Keep it."

(Both laugh)

M: He walked away, and we all said, "Oh, this shit is getting picked *up*."

N: *(Laughs again)* It's like a Selznick moment!

M: And then he later ended up giving me a lighter for some reason, and also one of the guys—Eric, I think, but then I'm pretty sure Eric lost his. So sorry, Donny O., some of your many dollars went to naught. I think I still have mine somewhere....

N: *(Narrator voice)* That is only the first of many spoilers that will be revealed in this salacious journal....

M: So. The story of how we met. We were between the second and third seasons, and the show was pretty popular at that point, but it hadn't taken on any sort of behemoth status.

N: I suppose it's worth mentioning that part of my philosophical makeup as a Chicago theater person— there's this defense mechanism by which we look down at things like the television sitcom as so much drivel.

M: May I interject? I remember walking down the sidewalk with a friend when I was in college at Northwestern, vowing passionately that I would NEVER do television, that it was beneath my dignity. I don't know what I thought I was going to do—Shakespeare? In the Vatican?

N: *(Laughs)*

M: It's so stupid. Because, PS, I love television, and I always have. I loved it when I was little, and I never stopped loving it, so why I had this bee in my bonnet about television is inexplicable.

N: It has something to do with defending the highbrow choice of pursuing theater.

M: Or movies. But of course that's all changed now. Because the majority of the best material is now on television.

How do we get back to our actual subject?

N: They told me, as an incentive when they set up the audition for the play, that they had Megan Mullally from *Will & Grace* as their lead in the play. And I said, "I know you think that's attractive, but I'm not interested in working with a person on television. I don't own a television, and I haven't for ten years." I'd never even seen *Friends* or *Seinfeld*.

M: Because you were sleeping on a couch in someone's basement!

N: I also didn't have electricity. Is that important?

M: *(Laughs)* Or indoor plumbing.

N: So I auditioned for the play, and I got the part, even though we found out later that the director hadn't wanted either one of us, for his own personal reasons.

M: It was funny, because we were the only ones who weren't members of the Evidence Room theater company. These two roles were offered to Nick and me, two big roles, and the director, who is clearly one sharp cookie, didn't want either one of us. But he did want all of the other people in the cast, some of whom were literally terrible.

N: The producer of the play and artistic director of the company, Bart DeLorenzo, was instrumental in convincing the director to hire both of us. When everyone showed up for the first read-through, I was actually there already. Part of the incentive for me, because I used to build all the scenery for my company in Chicago, the Defiant Theatre, was to help turn this beautiful warehouse building into a theater as we put up the show, so I signed on to help with that. I don't think they paid me . . . I guess that was part of my rent for living in the basement of a married couple who were in the company.

So I was there working, in a tool belt, building the walls, as we sat down for the first read-through. Apparently everybody was cowed by Megan because they were fans of her show, and rightly so.

M: Or maybe they'd never seen it; they just knew I was on a television show, period.

N: There was a weird standoffishness about it.

M: There was that theater snobbishness, or maybe people were going to reject me before I could reject them . . . ?

N: I think I'm more qualified in this instance, because I was one of them, one of the plebeians. And I think they were scared. It was the equivalent of "We're going to sit down and read the play like we always do, but Madonna is going to come and have a role."

M: *(Laughter)* Oh no. Well, I guess everything is relative! But you asked me at what stage *Will & Grace* was at that point. It was April of 2000 at the time, and in July of 2000 I found out I was nominated for my first Emmy. So I guess it actually was big enough to create at least a minor ruckus in the equity waiver world. . . .

N: So we did that first read-through. I love first read-throughs, because you get to find out—

M: We were sitting in a big circle, sitting in chairs in a big circle.

N: And if memory serves, if I may, I will say you were sitting at the noon position. I love first read-throughs because you get to find out what everybody's vibe is, and who's good, and who sucks. It's fun—it's like the first day of school. You find out who you're going to be friends with. I remember whatever preconceived notions I had, I was just gobsmacked by how funny, sharp, and smart you are. Now, you know that you would have shown up prepared—you wouldn't have just shown up and shit out a cold reading.

M: No, Mother doesn't do that.

N: *(Laughs)* So it was an absolute delight, as a cast member, to see that we were going to have a very strong leader.

M: And this is one of my few regrets—short-listed—I specifically remember I was wearing these giant red wooden platform sandals that had a rubber tread. I thought they were amazing. Several years later, I was cleaning out my closet, and our assistant at the time was there. I will not comment on his sexuality, but we got to that pair of shoes, and I said, "Should I keep these?" and he said, "Oh my god, NO!" And so I got really scared and threw them away.

N: I thought you weren't going to comment on his sexuality....

M: I threw them away, and I regret that, because those are the shoes I was wearing when I met my darling.

N: They were amazing. What was the name of that store on Melrose?

M: Yeah, they were from a place on Melrose. I can't remember what store it was, but I wish I still had them . . .

N: They were badass skips. I was so smitten with those shoes I wrote a lyric about them.
That was how we met. What was your first take? Do you remember what you thought of me and the role I assayed that day?

M: I had dutifully scanned the entire circle of the cast to see who I was going to have my fling with, because of course that's what you do the first day of rehearsal, if you're single. I'm sorry to say that my lord and master Nick Offerman did not make the first cut. He did not register on the fling-o-meter.

N: Did anyone else?

M: Well, I kind of felt like Leo did. And later on, you and I had a running gag that you also had scanned him to have a fling with. But that's old news. I don't know if there was anyone else. And even with Leo, the signal wasn't very strong.
I had always dated these certain types of guys, these pale, hairless, muscle-free, boyish . . . basically gay guys. Gay guys or rock drummers. Those were my two

categories. Nick did not fit into either of those categories, although I guess, conceivably, you could be a rock
drummer.

N: Thank you.

M: Nick is very manly. And I just didn't know what that
meant—I had no idea what that was.
So we read through the play, and it was . . . fine.

N: *(Laughs loudly)*

M: Everyone dispersed, and no one had said a word to me,
except for maybe the producer, Bart. But somehow I
was one of the last people to leave, and I just remember, like it was yesterday . . . Nick, do you remember it
that well? The actual meeting?

N: *(Emphatically)* Yes.

M: It's like it could be happening right this second.

N: Yes.

M: The space was a former bra factory, so it had concrete
floors and big factory windows with sunlight streaming in. The front half had been converted into a bar
where everybody would cavort before and after each
performance. The back half was these bleachers that
faced the stage area. We were exactly at the bleachers—
exactly halfway. I was walking out and I heard a voice.
I turned around, and there was this guy standing there,
and he said, "That was really fun. I think this is going
to be a blast." And I said, "Oh, yeah."

He said, "Hi, I'm Nick," and he put his hand out, and we shook hands.

I said, "Hi, I'm Megan," and he said, "Great job. I think this is going to be really cool. I'll see you around." And that was it.

N: She was SMITTEN.

M: *(Laughs)*

N: I can't believe she kept her feet. *(Laughs)*

M: It was nice. I didn't get any kind of feeling that he was trying to mack out on me or anything like that. I was just grateful that he had come up and introduced himself and made some pleasantries, because he was the only one. And then he turned out to be THE ONLY ONE FOR ME. End of book. We're done.

N: Boom.

M: G'night.

N: So it would be safe to say that we have good manners to thank for our inception.

M: That's right. Good country upbringings.

N: I do think, apropos of this book, it's worth noting that it wasn't love at first sight.

M: Uh, not for me! He was already in the bone zone. He just wasn't going to let on so soon.

N: *(Laughs loudly)* I had to go through some steps of self-realization before I could allow myself to be qualified to be in the bone zone. But what I want to point out—I think it's worth noting in terms of meeting the right person for you—is that the thing that first made us friends was that we really were attracted to what the other did. We recognized a kindred spirit in our performance styles, if you will. And senses of humor.

M: I have a slight amendment to that. There were a couple of musical numbers in the show that my character wasn't involved in, so I got to watch them. Nick did a lot of funny dancing, and he did some flips—some handsprings and stuff. Didn't you?

N: At least one. *(Laughs)*

M: And I thought, "That's cute." But I have to say that my first real spark with you was standing there on the stage, with the sun coming through those windows. We had been in the middle of rehearsing, but we weren't actively doing lines in that moment. We were on a break and we were just fucking around, doing bits with each other. And you made me laugh so hard—this wasn't the first time this had happened, this was, like, the seventh time. And I thought, "This guy really makes me laugh. Is he kind of sexy?"

N: There was a bit of confederacy between us. It was you and me against everybody.

M: Mm-hmm.

N: And so we'd often be off to the side, cracking each other up.

M: With our sidekick.

N: With our sidekick. *(Evil-ish laugh)* And you would say the filthiest things, and I couldn't wait to go home and tell my best friend, Pat, what Megan said today. "Can you believe this funny actress who's successful has a mouth this filthy? I think I may have found the one."

(Both laugh)

M: What else is there? There's nothing better than stupid, dirty humor.

N: No, there's really nothing better.

M: It's also the best way to bond with the cast. But there was a particular chemistry between me and Nick.

M: Let's address the sidekick factor.

N: I've learned it doesn't pay . . .

M: . . . I don't want to be mean.
It's just that it's important to note that Nick and I had a sidekick. Like all great romances, we had an impediment that needed to be overcome before our lips could touch. And the impediment came in the form of this person who had glommed on to . . . basically me, I guess, and then us, in that order. And we could not be rid of this person for one moment's time. So, ultimately, we had to resort to lying. I think we were in tech at that point, or in previews for the show.

We would have to say, "Oh, no, I'm just going home to-night, SOLO. I'm just going to hit the hay." And this person would watch us both like a hawk until we had each driven away. And then we'd have to take crazy back-road routes to get wherever we were going, and then meet up at, say . . .

N: A bordello. To have anal sex.

M: Why would we need to go to a bordello, though?

N: But we're getting a bit ahead of a proper retelling. Back up to my difficulties in just making you aware of my intentions.

M: Ah, yes. It's all coming back to me now. We had started flirting, and then there was a whole hilarious, classic, old-fashioned mix-up. This was 2000, pre–cell phone. At the beginning of any theatrical venture, there is a contact sheet for the cast so that if you have questions for a fellow cast member, you can contact them outside of work. But I had given my fax number because I didn't want any of those motherfuckers calling me at home. Around the time Nick and I had started laughing a lot and I was thinking, "Maybe he's cute," I was at home and ventured into a seldom-used corner of my apartment, the corner that housed my fax machine. And I saw a red light blinking. There was an answering machine on my fax, but no one ever left messages on it because it was A FAX MACHINE. So I never checked it. So I saw the blinking light, and I hit play, and there was this really charming message from Nick, who, at that moment, I realized for the first time, has a very pleasant speaking voice. He was asking me to come meet him at a club to see this band called Cowboy Nation. The message had been left at least a week before—it might have even been two weeks. It was a long time. And I thought, "Oops . . ." because I realized that this entire time he thought I'd been icing him.

The next day at rehearsal I said, "I just got your message, because that was my fax number." And we had a good laugh about that.

N: That was a good chuckle.

M: I had rushed into a lot of relationships in my past, and it hadn't worked out well. So I was bound and determined—because Nick is not fling material in any way, shape, or form—to not rush this process. I was a little unsure. Nick was different. He wasn't crazy, and he wasn't a bad guy. Those were some of the things I was used to, and I realized he wasn't any of those things, and I didn't know what to do about that. There was one night that I got into my car and started it up, and the passenger door opened, and Nick hopped into the passenger seat. *(Laughs)*

N: It was a Range Rover, so it was a jump. *(Laughs)*

M: Yes. He leapt into the seat with a lot of bravado, and I said, "Dude, whatever you think is going to happen right now is not going to happen. So you might want to pop on out of the Rover." And he did. He got out without a word.

N: No! There was a word. I remember clearly, because I was so scared to do that. Because of the weird social— I was living in someone's basement, and you were this amazing, shiny star. So I had to overcome the sort of social levels, the feeling that I was beneath you. So I jumped in, and you did say, "Back on out of the car," and I said, "OK, but I just have to ask you—this is going on, right? I'm not imagining this." And you were tough with me for a long time. You smiled and said, "We'll see. Nothing's going on right now." But you gave me enough encouragement that I continued to ply my troth.

M: That's funny because I didn't feel any social difference with us. On paper, you'd think I might. Nick wore these yellowish-gold overalls every day that he wrote people's addresses and phone numbers on—

N: There's a very practical reason for that.

M: Not being able to afford paper? The first time we went to dinner, he very ceremoniously unfurled his cloth napkin and tucked it into the bib of his overalls.

N: As I had learned from Jethro, a citizen of Beverly Hills . . .

M: *(Laughs)* . . . so you'd think I could ostensibly have had some sort of social something, but I didn't. I just liked Nick. I thought he was funny, and I thought he was nice. I didn't know what to make of him, because I'd never spent any time with a guy who was just a good guy like that.

N: Bone structure . . .

M: Those cheekbones! *(Laughs)* Those patrician cheekbones. That's what reeled me in.

But I'd never encountered anybody like that. All this stuff—living on somebody's couch, tucking his napkin into his overalls—it didn't occur to me for a second that any of it was a strike against him or something. He seemed very confident. And he had a lot of personal dignity, much more so than every other guy I had dated, guys who were, on paper, much more quote-unquote sophisticated.

Early on, and this is really important, after we had become a couple, after I made him jump through fifteen thousand hoops to get to the puss—so post-puss, when we were a couple—we went out to dinner one night. I said, "You know, I've heard that a lot of men have a hard time being involved with a woman who is more overtly successful than they are. I have a job right now, and I'm making money—is that going to be a problem for you?" And he looked me in the eye and said, "You know what? I've never had any money, and I've always lived like a king." And I thought, "Jesus, good answer." He's rich in spirit. *(Excited voice)* But now *he's* got a lot of money!

N: Ha-ha!

M: Yet again, the joke's on . . . somebody.

N: Now I'm rich in the finest Jordache jeans . . .

I moved in with Megan. Was it after the play closed?

M: No . . . not exactly. Here's how this all breaks down. I held Nick at bay for an unreasonably long period of time for a variety of reasons, the primary reason being that I had rushed into a lot of relationships in the past, and I didn't want to do that again. So I kind of went overboard—overcompensated—with Nick. We rehearsed, we flirted, we had the sidekick, we went to dinner and he tucked his napkin in. On the way out of the napkin restaurant, heading back to the car, Nick surreptitiously took my hand as we went down an escalator, and he linked his fingers through mine, and I had little butterflies.

N: Escalator hand-holding. Boom.

M: The escalator hand-hold was the first move, and it worked. It was just simple and romantic. Nick is not a big operator. It's great, because I've been with him for eighteen years now, and I never have to worry that he's out banging somebody else. Because he doesn't have it in him. He's not that kind of person.

N: It's a nice quality in a marriage. It does come in handy.

M: It's an advantage.
  We had the hand-holding. We then arranged to somehow steal away from the sidekick and meet for drinks at the Red Lion in Silver Lake with a couple of Nick's boyfriends, because I think Nick secretly wanted to see what the boyfriends had to say. If I'm not reading into that.

N: No, that's correct.

M: We went and had drinks with them. I only drank wine, and the wine there was AMAZING, and then we dropped off his friends. Music was playing—I think it was Beck.

N: Beck, "Beautiful Way."

M: We kissed, and I was saying, "No, we shouldn't kiss," because we were in rehearsals, and I was thinking we couldn't be involved during the run of the show, and it was going to be a nightmare...

N: It was unseemly.

M: Not to put too fine a point on it, but you're not supposed to fuck where you work. But things happen.

N: Cupid had another idea...

(Both laugh)

M: It turned into kind of a make-out sesh. Like a thirty-minuter.

N: We kept replaying the song—I'd say ten times.

M: We kept playing the song over and over again. Oh my god... it was nice. It was sweet.
Our next rendezvous was at this little place on Franklin. We sat at a front table near the window. Deep thoughts were exchanged. We had a longer make-out session by my car. Then it became a regular sort of thing.

So we were making out on the reg. But that was it. Finally, Nick was like, "You know, I left my . . . galoshes . . . at your apartment." But he'd never been to my apartment. He was trying to finagle some way to get over there.

Sidebar: He drove a rusted-out red ragtop . . .

N: Chevy Cavalier.

M: What was the year?

N: Probably 1993.

M: Mm-hmm . . . And he also had a real beater of a motorcycle, and I loathe motorcycles. But in whichever vehicle, he eventually got over to my apartment.

(To Nick) I don't even think I let you come in the first time.

The second time I let him come in, but he couldn't go past the living room. Then he slept over, but he had to sleep on the couch. Then he made it to the bed for make-out times, but I wouldn't let him *sleep* in the bed. He had to go back out and sleep on the couch. Then ultimately, of course, he got to sleep in the big-boy bed.

This was the beginning of us living together, because you never went back to your apartment. The first time you came over to my apartment, that was it. Even though I wouldn't let you into any rooms but the living room. And that includes the bathroom. *(Laughs)*

N: There was no question. I had been looking for the woman of my dreams, with whom I could trust my devotion, and I found you. I would have fucking still slept on the couch for years, because, great—if you'll let me adore you, I'll be here. *(Laughs)*

M: Women who read this are going to be murdering their boyfriends right now. With their words. Not literally. A lot of women reading this are going to be having a good, hard think right about now. Because there are not too many men like you.

N: I come by it honest. My parents are pictures of fidelity. They have incredible integrity and character. I'm sure some of that comes from them. It's not like I'm so noble or something—I simply knew.

M: He had stick-to-it-iveness.

N: There was no thinking involved. My internal clock, my alarm went off and said, "You're done looking."

(Both laugh)

M: As much as I was keeping him at bay—and as slowly as I was taking things—all I wanted was to be in love, and be happy, and have a life with someone. I always thought that someday I would find a really great person to spend my life with. But I was forty-one at this point, and . . . a sort of once-bitten, twice-shy aspect was in operation. But that was my hope, my fervent desire. By taking it really slow, that was my way of protecting myself and making sure that there wasn't some other shoe that was going to hilariously drop and blow everything up. And there wasn't.

On the Fourth of July, Nick and I went to see Glen Campbell at the Hollywood Bowl. It was a really nice night.

N: The Hollywood Bowl is a beautiful outdoor amphitheater. The audience sits on the side of a hill, up in the Hollywood Hills. It was one of those moments that felt like what I dreamed Los Angeles would be like. Glen Campbell's playing a show, the stars are out, it smells amazing, the climate is immaculate, I'm with the love of my life, and . . . it's fucking Glen Campbell.

M: *(Laughs)* We had bought a blanket at the Hollywood Bowl's little store. It was a little chilly, and we bought a lap blanket that was very corny.

N: I loved it.

M: I bought this blanket because I knew Nick was going to go crazy over it, because it had a big American eagle on it. It was hideous.

N: *(Laughs)*

M: But there was also something really beautiful about it. And Nick did love it, and it became this big thing. Years later, cleaning out the garage, that blanket got disposed of—by the same assistant who nixed the red shoes, PS—and when Nick found out it was gone, he was devastated. Someday, I hope to replace it, because I didn't fully realize the depths of Nick's attachment to it until it got dumped.

N: That loss was a nadir.

M: Oh man. We should have kept the blanket. And the red shoes. I think someday, somehow, they'll come back to us.

N: I'd like to see you in just the blanket and the red shoes.

M: How about just the red shoes?

N: I'll take it.

M: So we sat there with our blanket and listened to Glen Campbell. I don't know if everybody's dream concert would be Glen Campbell, but that was another thing. Nick and I have a similar sensibility. That's an important quality in a relationship—liking the same things. I know there are many a couple who are very happy despite having different interests, likes, and dislikes. But for me, it sure makes it easier when you can really enjoy the *Bachelor* franchise together.
So Glen Campbell played, and he was great. Then after Glen Campbell, because it was the Fourth of July, the LA Philharmonic, or parts thereof, played all of these very rousing *(Sings)* "Ba ba, ba ba ba, ba ba ba ba ba BA!"

N: John Philip Sousa.

M: We'd met in April. This was July Fourth. We'd been making out for, like, two months at this point. At the high point of the fireworks, at the ultimate moment of this night, I turned to Nick, brought him close, and whispered in his ear, "I want you to be my boyfriend."

Because as strange as it may sound, we weren't even officially boyfriend and girlfriend. I hadn't even gone that far yet. And the next night, July fifth . . .

N: There were more fireworks. *(Laughs)*

M: He was introduced to m'puss.

N: And now you're reading our book. Welcome.

M: To be followed with a giant photograph of my puss.

BAKE AMAZING COOKIES

BY NICK

AS I AM A HAPPILY MARRIED PERSON, MANY SINGLE FRIENDS
and acquaintances have asked me for advice on how to meet
a mate. Upon investigation, I learned that many of the afore-
mentioned friends had been trying to find consensual attraction using online dating services. You know, like Tinder for
straight people, Grindr for gay men, and that new one called
Attractor (for lonely farmers, I assume). One pal who shall
remain nameless (Luis) was weighing the idea of attending a
local baking workshop, where the attendees were purported
to learn to bake "amazing cookies." I said to him, "Let me
stop you right there . . . *Of course you should go to that.*" The
best way to find a mate who will stick is for them to see you
doing something that you love.

Elsewhere in this volume you will have read about how far
"up" I married, so you will have to agree that I stand as con-
clusive proof of this idea. To refresh: When I first met Megan at
rehearsal for a play we were both in, she had just finished the

first two seasons of *Will & Grace* and was about to win her first Emmy. I was literally living in my friend's unfinished dirt-and-stone basement in exchange for turning it into a habitable space so that it could be rented to civilized humans. I could flagrantly and flamboyantly urinate in the middle of the room and by the next day you couldn't tell where it had occurred. Yes, I agree that is awesome, but that was really the only good thing about living there besides the price. Clearly we were existing at very different levels of prosperity, as measured by personal hygiene, if nothing else. But when I met Megan that first day, I was also helping the theater company carpenter build a stage in its new warehouse building, so I was wearing a tool belt and I was covered in a patina of sweat and sawdust and satisfaction. I have to believe that whatever glow she saw coming off of my ursine features must have played a substantial role, even subliminally, in her eventual decision to roll the dice on a relationship with me.

So I told my friend, of course you should go to a cookie-baking class, because, number one, you will be walking into some cool loft space that will be warm and sweetly redolent of baking cookies. Number two, there will be no married people there, but there will undoubtedly be other single people hoping to assist their own mating games tossing around phrases like "mouthfeel" and "eggbeater" and "moist batter." "Make sure you have greased your muffin cups." Come on, Luis! At some point in the proceedings you are sure to participate in the group chewing mouthfuls of glorious cookies, smiling at one another and saying, "Mmmm," and nodding. If you can't engage a new love friend out of that scenario, then I don't know what to do with you.

And, worst-case scenario, if you don't find your true love there, you will have merely succeeded in tricking yourself into baking amazing cookies. That's the best part of this technique. Get out of your house, get off of your phone, then go and participate in things that thrill you. Maybe it's a softball team, maybe it's playing bluegrass music, maybe it's a flooring seminar at the home improvement center (just embonered myself)—it doesn't matter what it is, so long as you like it. When people see you doing something you deeply enjoy, they see you at your most attractive.

Don't go to events where the stated objective is to find romance. A spark is much more likely to catch fire when the participants are not lined up scrutinizing the hearth for the first hint of smoke. To my recollection, I have been on only two actual dates in my life, pre-Megan, yet I have had a healthy and fruitful record in relationships with ladies, ending in this current bountiful harvest of eighteen years and counting. The vast majority of these romantic liaisons, including my marriage, were born in the theater, where we were able to very deeply observe one another engaging in a very vulnerable version of something we love: acting.

You know, that's not bad since I'm currently in this advice-giving mood. Looking for love? Head to the theater. There's theater everywhere, and you can audition for shows, sure, but there are a million other things you can do. Build scenery, design and sew costumes, hang lights, create special effects, help in the lobby, help with advertising and promotion, raise money, write and perform music—shit, you can sweep! You'd be surprised how many establishments in life can be infiltrated if you stand around until you can sweep or take out the trash. I see it all so clearly now. Theater is the answer. Or cookies. Boom.

The secret is to take a good look at your inner garden and see what you can nourish, be it fruit or vegetable, weavable or smokable, and then cultivate it. Like a real garden, it will take patience and learning. Whatever takes root, water it, encourage it to grow and flower and fully bush. Luscious fruit comes in many forms. Go do something delicious and see if you don't end up getting kissed to boot.

CHAPTER 2

You're Just Trying To Get In On The Action Because Your Family Is Like A Norman Rockwell Painting

Nick: Families is the topic.

Megan: We both have families. So technically we have that in common. But we have really different families.

N: I come from a big family. On my mom's side, she was one of four kids, so her parents and three siblings formed a pretty large extended family, all living in the town of Minooka, Illinois. Growing up, there were about twenty-four of us, and now that number is up into the thirties. Every household was pretty similar—very hardworking, salt of the earth. Everyone in the entire family is a public servant—teacher, librarian, nurse, paramedic, farmer—with the exception of my brother, who brews beer, and is thus considered the king of the family. I'm the only black sheep.

M: I'm an only child. My whole family is dead—except for my mom, who's ninety-six, and my father's brother, my uncle Taylor, who is eighty-seven or eighty-eight. They're both wonderful. And I have a few cousins, some of whom are acceptably within the parameters of sanity. But the hilarious part of Nick's and my family dynamic is that Nick's family is, by and large, normal, whereas my family were all completely insane. So that's a jumping-off point. And Nick's family are also alive, so that's a plus.

N: My family is very Midwestern. They're very hardworking. They have an amazing work ethic and sense of neighborliness. Everyone takes care of one another, both within the family and within the community. Whatever few hardships they have are born of perhaps repressing emotion and the occasional overindulgence in food and drink.

They work hard, but they don't talk a lot about their feelings. There's a great familial love, which gives a great feeling of security.

M: Nick's family is really nice. And they're all funny, which you won't be surprised to hear. Plus they're readers—his sisters, Laurie and Carrie, are a librarian and a teacher, respectively, and Nick's mom, Cathy, is a voracious reader. That's something I can really relate to, because I like to move my eyeballs across a typed page as well. Aside: That's not a good phrase. Correction: I like to read.

N: *(Laughs)* I'll take it. I, too, like to read! I like to move my eyeballs across the page!

M: That does sound like something you would say. *(Laughs)*
Two things. I'm fifty-nine, so you wouldn't think it was that unusual that a lot of my family are gone, but it's been the case for lo these many years. My father's side of the family were all clearly certifiable. So that was never in question. But I've recently come to find out that my mother's side of the family—with a few notable exceptions, which include my mother's mother, otherwise known as Granny—were also completely insane. Funny story.

N: I should mention, though, that my dad's family experience was closer to some of the aspects of your family experience. His parents were divorced . . .

M: Oh my god, what? This book is going to go through the roof! Your grandparents were divorced?! I can't compete with that . . .

N: My granny was a pretty sad character. She was an alcoholic, and very lonely.

M: Okay, everyone in my family is either an alcoholic and/ or has some kind of substance abuse problem except for my mom and, like, two other people. It runs the gamut in my family. Suicide, sociopathy, incest ... it's a scream. It's the stuff of comedy. Of the comedy book we're writing together.

N: *(Laughs)* I wasn't competing ...

M: ... You're just trying to get in on the action because your family is like a Norman Rockwell painting.

N: By comparison, the happy hobbits of the Roberts family ...

M: *(Laughs)* The basic bottom line is that our families are very different. And yet we kind of grew up in the same environment. Even though Nick is twelve—I'm going to say eleven and a half—years younger than I am, he grew up in Minooka, which was a small farm town at the time, and I grew up in Oklahoma City, which is the capital of Oklahoma, but when I was growing up, it had a small-town vibe that was similar to Nick's upbringing. Not quite the same, of course, because Nick actually worked on his uncle's farm. I did not work on anyone's farm, unfortunately. I went to private school for twelve years and went to the mall.

N: With regard to the marriages I grew up under the influences of, it was Grandpa Mike and Grandma El, who ran the farm and were the source of all the fun. We had enough people to play softball together, and we'd have huge family meals. It was a great example.

And seeing how each of my mom's siblings, and my own parents, handled their families taught me a lot of lessons in terms of communicating and getting along with people. They were never overt: I didn't go to college thinking, "I'm well equipped to get along with others!" But in hindsight, I realize I do get along with others well. I thank my mom and dad and larger family that I can get thrown in with a group and get along with everybody, pretty much.

M: Nick's parents have a really great relationship, and it's so nice to see. His father is cute and romantic with his mother. He's always talking about how pretty she is and putting his arm around her. It's very sweet, and I think that Nick gets some of his romantic side from that.

My mom was very supportive of me when I was growing up, and always tried to maintain a positive attitude. My father was an actor who never had much success. He was mostly busy drinking and cheating on my mom, although that wasn't his professional trade. His trade was acting, and he did a few things here and there, but mostly theater around Oklahoma and Texas. He was a contract player at Paramount in the 1950s for a brief time, but he never got a big part, although he is in the pilot episode of *The Twilight Zone*—he's a reporter, and he has maybe one or two lines. But he never managed to really get a toehold.

N: That's like a sci-fi story to me, though. You could be saying, "My dad spent a couple years as a Knight of the Round Table. He just jousted against . . ."

M: *(Laughs)* Well, he *was* very exotic. He was very actory and flamboyant. When I was in second grade, he bought a 1937 Rolls-Royce Phantom III, and he would drive it around Oklahoma City wearing an ascot. And he was a straight guy. Or straight-ish. I can't believe he didn't get murdered. So that was an accomplishment.

My mom spent a lot of time trying to encourage him, encouraging him to follow his dreams. And once it became clear that I had been born in a top hat and tap shoes, she was extremely supportive of me as well. I started ballet at six, and anything creative I wanted to pursue, she would encourage. I think she had a slight touch of the stage mother, but not nearly as bad as some mothers have it. I was in a ballet company from eighth through twelfth grades, so I saw a lot of stage mothers. I would say she was in the thirtieth percentile.

N: Knowing your mother, I would say she would be effective without being obnoxious.

M: Yes, although she did brag about me constantly. People still tell me that she'd stop them in the Crescent Market and talk about me to whomever she could get her hands on.

N: One difference between Minooka and Megan's neighborhood in Oklahoma City is that the Crescent Market was carpeted!

M: Red carpeting with a fountain inside! It was pretty fancy.

N: They had, like, nine kinds of sardines.

M: Look, it was swanky.

N: It was the bomb.

M: I think because my dad could be, shall we say, unpleasant to be around, I spent most of my childhood upstairs in my bedroom with the door closed, making up dramatic dances. My parents had a couple of records of instrumental movie themes. I'd put on a record and work on one song until I had it perfected, and then I'd show it to my mother. And it would invariably involve me dancing around, having a mad scene, and then dying of love. Which is basically what I do in my day-to-day life now.

Even though I was doing all of that, I was doing it alone. I had friends on the block, but I spent a lot of time alone. I was extremely shy and inhibited for many years, well into *Will & Grace*. It took me a long time to shed my self-consciousness and inhibitions. It seems hard to believe, yet you must believe me.

I had this burning desire to express myself in a creative way at a very early age. I knew every song on the radio. Every time a song came on, I'd sing along. I can still sing every lyric now, even if I haven't heard the song in a million years. As for dancing, occasionally I'd go-go dance on a stool for my mom and my dad, which is just as crazy as it sounds. On a stool. I'd do the pony.

While all this was happening, I was also afraid of everything. Because of the way my father was, I never felt like I could do anything right. Everything I did seemed to throw him into a rage. So I tried to be perfect and never make any mistakes. You know, the usual.

I said that my father being an actor was exotic. And it was. Everyone in Oklahoma thought my father was exotic. But my father would have been exotic in the middle of Hollywood Boulevard. He was also extremely funny when he wanted to be. And in an unexpected way. He'd take chances with his humor—he'd do a bit and he'd commit to it. Which is something Nick does, too. He'll F with people and really dig in without any fear. Even with total strangers. I can't do that. I'll start a bit and then immediately say, "I'm just kidding!"

But Nick grew up in a small town, and his father wasn't a flamboyant, extroverted actor. They had five movies on VHS—which ones were they?

N: *Sound of Music, Singin' in the Rain, Seven Brides for Seven Brothers, Bridge on the River Kwai,* and *The Quiet Man.*

M: But they had this one video . . . *(Both laugh)* There's a home movie of Nick at a family function—someone is panning around, and they're all shyly smiling at the camera. And then there's Nick, bouncing back and forth from one hip to the other, both arms up, pointing at his head, at his face, like, "Look at Me! I'm Here! Here I Am! I'm Doing It!"

But he didn't know what he was doing. He was trying to do showbiz, I think. But he didn't even know. It was like Helen Keller: W-A-T-E-R! But he didn't know what he was doing. He just knew that he desperately needed to express himself and be recognized.

N: I think it's an interesting contrast. You say you never broke the rules, Miss Goody Two-Shoes. . . .

M: Never colored outside the lines . . .

N: Partly because you were terrified of discipline.

M: Discipline in my house was not like discipline in other houses. Just irate rage, just rage and screaming.

N: A drunken rage was a substitute for discipline.
The more Wendell Berry that I read, and the older I get and see how people are, the more I am grateful to my parents and really respect them. Because it's not like it was easy—they worked their asses off at being these two apple-cheeked Midwesterners, out in the middle of the country, with a house my dad fucking rolled there on a flatbed. They raised four kids. I remember one time my dad was yelling, which was rare—he's very taciturn—and he stormed out the front door, which was rare, because we used the back door, in the kitchen, and I remember my mother standing there watching, crying. And I thought, "Holy shit, Mom's crying about something with Dad. That's fucking crazy—I didn't know that was an option in this house."

M: That blows my mind, that it was a crazy isolated incident for you.

N: I thought, "What's going on? I didn't know they had that channel."

M: That was, like, THE CHANNEL at my house. There was only one channel.

N: Just imagine, you and me, in our twenties, with four kids. *(Laughs)* I'm sure we'd give it a hell of a good go, but it really makes me respect them and their efforts. They were so amazing. I required the most discipline, by far, of the four of us kids . . .

M: What would you do?

N: I would never burn the barn down. I was just pushing their buttons. I was always trying to figure out what I could get away with.

M: *(Singing in a funny voice)* Not a lot has changed. . . .

N: And so, traditionally, my mom would discipline me with a yardstick. Until she broke the yardstick over my butt and we both started cracking up, and then she chased me down. But very rarely, my dad would take me into the mudroom, and he would hold me by—whatever that ligament is connecting the neck to the shoulder—and give me a really low talking-to. And that was so much scarier. He never raised his hand to us, which I have to say I really admire.

M: I can't believe your mom went at you with a yardstick! That's surprising. The irony is . . . Well, keep going.

N: That was quite gentle! It was a humane version of the options available to her.

M: Can I just say that the irony is that you were phys-
ically spanked with a yardstick, whereas I was only
actually spanked once by my father—it was like half of
a spanking—but I was emotionally abused 24/7 for my
entire childhood? So I guess I would rather have had a
few spankings with the yardstick.

N: It's an interesting dichotomy.

M: Yeah, it's a real gas.

N: Most of the time I was well behaved. We all had our
chores. We had jobs inside and outside of the house,
and we were all avid athletes and musicians and all
kinds of stuff, but I was always pushing the bound-
aries of authority, and I don't know where that came
from. It was something intrinsic to me. It wasn't until I went to college, and was out from under their
roof . . . I called my dad pretty early on, a few weeks
into college, and said, "I'm sorry I was such an ass-
hole the whole time. Now that I'm balancing my own
checkbook and paying my own bills, all of a sudden it
all hits home. Thank you."
I must have been so unbearable. But they were patient
and stuck with me. I'd get in trouble for lying about
something or ditching school, and they'd say, "You
just have to do your work and be honest, and that's it."
And my life has succeeded, so far as it has, through
those incredibly simple lessons.

M: Nobody ever said anything like that to me at home.
But I got a lot of discipline at school. I went to the same
school for twelve years. It was a great school called

Casady. And I was in this ballet company. So between the very strict private school that I went to and the strict, incredibly regimented world of a ballet company, I got a ton of discipline. *(Laughs)* I'm very thankful for both of those things. My mother overcompensated for my terror-filled childhood by never making me do anything. When I got to college, I got into bed the first night in my dorm room—with my roommate in the other bed—and I got out the next day and looked at it and thought, "Huh . . ." I never fucking even tried. I didn't even have a concept of how to make a bed. It was a complete and utter mystery to me.

I know how to make a bed now. Now I'm the other way.

N: You're a goddess.

M: You could bounce a quarter off of our entire house.

N: You CURATE a bed.
Since I've known you, there have been . . . one, two, three . . . seven home beds . . .

M: I own a whorehouse! Not a lot of people know that.

N: In the brothel, the beds are immaculate. And that bleach substitute really works.
As your spaces are your works of art, the bed is the focus—I'm sure there's a cool art term for it—like Mona Lisa's face. Between the bedding, and the design of the whole thing, and the comfort of the pillows.

M: I feel like we've talked about beds a lot.

N: You mean this chapter is not "Beds"?

M: Thinking through all of this right now, it's so complicated for me to talk about my upbringing because I've never spoken about it publicly. I've never even mentioned that my father was an alcoholic, much less everything else.

So it's so interesting to hear Nick talk about his family. And I know his family, but to hear some of the things he said—that seeing his parents have one argument completely blew his mind and he didn't know that could happen. And that he was disciplined in such a Norman Rockwell-y kind of way . . . Even Norman Rockwell did paintings of children being spanked. I didn't have that at all. I grew up in a fucking Fellini movie.

My mom put on this face of normalcy and thought she had shielded me from all these things. But she couldn't have really thought that. I was her accomplice in some of the investigations of my father's infidelities, and anyway . . . it's just sad.

Therefore, I'm so glad that not only do I have Nick, I have Nick's family, who are so normal, but not in the boring way. Just well-adjusted.

N: They're steady and constant.

M: *(Agrees)* They're steady and constant. They're also extremely warm and genuine.

N: Here's a hard right. My family—I'm not sure, honestly, I guess Mom's parents must have gone to the Methodist church, because Aunt Dee and Uncle Dan go to the Methodist church, and our family is Catholic. So it must have been my mom stepping over when she married my dad. But the whole family grew up going to church. I would say that my family members are some of the most exemplary people, living lives that would be considered Christian, but only through their actions. Nobody ever mentioned any church stuff, anywhere, except a possible mention of God or heaven or hell, and in a proverbial way, "If you keep that up, you won't be going to heaven." But even that would be super rare.

Today, none of my siblings go to church. It didn't take with us. We all stopped going to church the minute we left their house.

M: Don't blow your wad. We have a whole religion chapter coming up.

N: Then I'll leave it at that. The whole family went to church, even though nobody was demonstrably "churchy" in any way. I learned so much more about decency and how to treat my fellow person from the actions of my fellow family members than I ever did from listening to a priest.

M: I don't know who I learned all that stuff from. The problem with my mom is that I watched her take all this abuse from my dad every day and not leave him. So that's tough. It's hard to say, "My mom was across-the-boards amazing!" She is pretty darn amazing, though. And unconditionally supportive, which made up for a lot.

My grandmother, her mother, was the real thing. Salt of the earth. She was born in 1888. She lived to be ninety-nine, and traveled by covered wagon.

N: Even in the '60s!

M: *(Laughing)* The jokes, they're flying!
She was a great example. My mother's father died when she was seventeen, so I obviously never met him. He, apparently, was pretty great, too.

N: Seems like you came out pretty good, though.

M: *(Laughs)* I'm still learning. But I have Nick Offerman as my example, day in and day out, and that's about as good as it gets.

N: *(Crisp fart noise)*

M: But I've had to learn a lot of things along the way. Everything was very compartmentalized for me. I was so together in terms of my creative life. I taught myself to sing by singing along with records. My parents had Barbra Streisand and Judy Garland records. My parents were two gay men, apparently. I would pick one Barbra Streisand song, and I would sing it over and over again until I could sing it exactly like the record. I was just driven to do it. I loved it so much. I must have had some innate ability, coupled with the discovery that I could really express myself emotionally through singing in a way I couldn't in real life. That probably drove me subconsciously in some way, but I also genuinely loved it. And I do believe that children are born with certain proclivities, and I guess that was one of mine.

So I had honed my talents in all these different areas. But as a human being, I was way behind. I had no idea what anything meant, the important things in life. I thought that because I knew how to sing and do other creative things, that meant I was a well-rounded person. But I didn't know about anything else, about how to be a conscious person living in the world.

N: Well, somebody did a very good job. Maybe Casady, your school, had something to do with it? I feel like you have really good manners, and I feel like we are great checks and balances for each other. In different circumstances, we say, "Hey, did you send a thank-you to that person?" I don't feel like I've got anything on you when it comes to being neighborly.

M: *(Laughs)* I guess I was cheerful and polite. There's something about Oklahoma City, or at least the area where I grew up, the people there are SO nice. Nick can attest to it.

N: Hear, hear!

M: There is such a generosity, and a neighborliness, and a real willingness to help others. In the middle of urban LA or the middle of Manhattan, you don't see it as much. It's a genuine Southern comfort. A selflessness.

N: When we talk about our upbringings, I think that's what's most similar. We both grew up in a Midwestern feeling, for lack of a better term. Where everybody had the attitude of "we're all in this together."

This is also a good segue to something I really wanted to bring up, which is that, if we're talking about family, your group of friends continues to be as devoted as any family, which I think should be discussed.

M: I still have a lot of friends who I went to school with in Oklahoma City, many who still live there and a couple of people who live outside Oklahoma City. I've known them since first grade in a few notable cases, and others I've known since sixth or seventh grade. We all went to school together all that time, and I've been friends with them all along. It's a very solid, core, staunch group of friends. Nick can't get over it, because he doesn't have close friends that he's known consistently through his life, especially from such an early age.

So every time we go to Oklahoma City, we have this great group of friends there, and I think that it's a testament to my mom. My mom wanted to have ten children. My mom and my father tried for nine years to get pregnant, and they finally got pregnant with me. Then, after I was born, my mom had five miscarriages. So she didn't get to have the ten children. They had talked about adopting at one point, but decided to get divorced instead.

So this group of friends I have in Oklahoma City now—almost without exception, all of their mothers passed away at a relatively young age. So a lot of these friends are very close to my mom. She's been like a mother to so many of them, plus a couple of girls from my ballet company. It's weird that a lot of my friends' mothers died at a younger age, and my mom—who had so wanted a lot of children—was the mother who was still there. My mother is still in the same house that she's lived in for fifty-three years. She's just there, my mom. She's still there.

N: The feeling I get from this group of your friends is the feeling I get from my family. It's moving, what they put out—you call, they come. Even when you DON'T call, they come. They maintain a fidelity with your mom, and with you, that's really touching.

M: We talk about it a lot, but I'm glad you brought it up. My friends provide more of a balance for me, and make up for some of the lack of family. Melinda and Rhonda and Chip, in particular, they're like the triumvirate at the center of all that. On any given day, Rhonda could be over there, doing something nice for my mom. I'm not saying my mom asked them to do something—she never would—but they're over there, bringing her a milkshake. Repairing something that needs to be repaired.

N: Acting like family.

M: Yes, acting like family.

N: When I was growing up, there were five households— my mom and her three siblings, and their parents' farm makes the fifth. I should add that my dad has a brother and a sister, but we just didn't see them as much. Maybe on special occasions and holidays. But my dad's dad, Ray, was the mayor of Minooka.

M: *Literally* the mayor of Minooka.

N: He was a constant presence. He was instrumental. He would be at all of the Roberts family things.

When you have five households, which is now ten or twelve, you never have to go to a restaurant. For birthdays and holidays, you just switch houses. So Christmas this year is at Aunt Dee's house. Or we'd have coffee Sunday—whoever is available on a Sunday gathers at the designated house to get the news. And so it was a HUGE deal when we would go to a fucking McDonald's, never mind a real sit-down restaurant, which would be like somebody won the Olympics or something.

And so that really gave an element of fantasy to when our families would go to the movies—which was a huge deal, because you had to drive to another town to do it. Let alone go to a Cubs game, which was the pinnacle of our year.

M: Going to Chicago was like going to Bali or something.

N: It was insane! And it turns out it's, like, forty-five minutes from Minooka to Lake Shore Drive. It's like a trip to the grocery store in Los Angeles.

It was that quality that, when it came time to look at colleges . . . Financially, it only made sense, since I got good grades and I qualified for a scholarship, it was much cheaper for me to go to state schools. I wanted to be an entertainer, so I thought, *(Musing)* "I believe people go to this city called New York. There's also this Los Angeles place . . ." But the thought of one of those would be like going to the moon. It would be completely unheard of for anyone in Minooka.

M: And conversely, I spent two summers in Manhattan studying at the School of American Ballet, which is New York City Ballet's school. It's in the Juilliard building, but it's not part of Juilliard. And it's next door to Lincoln Center.

My mom went with me both summers, because I was only sixteen and seventeen. We rented an apartment with another girl from my ballet company in Oklahoma City and her mom. My mom would take me to museums, to the ballet, and to see Broadway shows. So from the time I was sixteen, I got this incredible cultural education. I can't tell you how many times I saw Baryshnikov dance, and Gelsey Kirkland, and Nureyev. All of the greats, and all of the Russian dancers.

My mom was unstoppable. One morning in the *New York Times* there was a review of a new little show called *A Chorus Line*. It was a rave review, on the front page of the Arts section. Just this huge, amazing review. My mother said, "We have to see it tonight."

So, right then and there, we get in the elevator, hail a cab, and she takes me down to Times Square, to Shubert Alley, marches up to the box office and says, "I need two tickets for the show tonight."

The guy behind the ticket window burst out laughing. "You can't get a ticket for this show—this show is sold out until the end of time."

My mom—who was the real actor in the family—says, "I have brought my tiny, small daughter all the way from Oklahoma to see this show, and if you can't get her a ticket, then you will personally be ruining this child's life." I think she basically intimated that I might be dying of something.

And suddenly we were front row center in the balcony for the first show after opening night.

N: She got you dope house seats!

M: She got me the *producer's* house seats. There were a few times my mother managed actual tears to try to finagle something for me. She did that a few different times. It's some kind of trick she learned on the mean streets of Greater Tulsa.

So I had all this exposure to culture. But New York was dangerous then. Seventy-second Street—it was like Beirut. Nobody EVER went that far uptown. Central Park was completely off-limits. You couldn't set a toe in Central Park, even in the daytime. It was just discarded needles everywhere and crazy shit going down. One time a guy chased me down 66th Street between Columbus and Central Park West at three o'clock in the afternoon. We were at a full sprint. I finally ducked into the ABC building and asked for help. And this sounds like a joke, but it's not: Ten years later I shot my first television show—*The Ellen Burstyn Show*—in that same building.

But I did get this great exposure to dance and theater. It was amazing.

N: It was amazing. I think if my parents had taken me to see Baryshnikov . . . then I could have had a career in ballet.

M: It's not too late!

N: It was stolen from me.

M: *(Laughs)* I was also allowed to watch a lot of television, which I loved, and I still love. My mom and I watched shows like *Mary Hartman, Mary Hartman,* and that show completely blew my mind. Nothing like that had existed previously. I can't believe they even showed it in Oklahoma City. It was very avant-garde, not bright and shiny like other shows at the time. There wasn't even a laugh track. And the crazy soap *Dark Shadows,* which was totally nuts and I was completely obsessed with. It was a sort of dark-comedy soap opera about a vampire, next to, like, *General Hospital,* in the middle of the afternoon. It was insane. Also, the music that I would sing along to—when I hear songs from the '60s and '70s now, I think, "Oh my god, these songs are so filthy!" But I had no idea that they were at the time, and I was singing along in the car at full blast with my mom. Either she thought it was funny or she didn't get that they were dirty—I don't know. But I remember singing "Fancy" about a thousand times, which is a song about a mother who sells her daughter into prostitution, but everything works out great! So I guess it's the perfect Mother's Day anthem.

She wasn't conservative with me. I had a deal with her when I was really little. I loved Carol Burnett, who was on CBS on Monday nights at nine, which was my bedtime. So on Mondays I went to bed at eight, and I slept for an hour, and then my mom would wake me up, and I would watch Carol Burnett, and then go back to sleep.

I really studied everyone on and everything about Carol Burnett and also *Mary Hartman, Mary Hartman*, that first really weird comedic TV show. In retrospect, I wouldn't have thought my mom would have liked shows like *Mary Hartman, Mary Hartman* because she dressed like Nancy Reagan and was pretty mah-jonggy, but I think ultimately my mom had really good taste when it came to pop culture. We also watched *Laugh-In* religiously. That was a more mainstream show but super groundbreaking for the time.

I always loved comedy. I would get my mom to buy me comedy albums: Redd Foxx, Bill Cosby, the Smothers Brothers, Phyllis Diller, Bob Newhart, et cetera. I don't think any other kids I knew listened to comedy records. It never dawned on me that I might one day have a career in comedy. I just liked comedy, and the weirder the better.

N: My dad is uncanny in his ability to name actors, up to about 1975. He could see any movies from the 1950s on and identify all the actors. He also knew a lot of singers. My family would watch *M*A*S*H* and *Taxi,* the great shows, and my dad and I would bond over characters like Jim Ignatowski on *Taxi,* or Jackie Gleason. We loved character actors. There was a guy named Jack Elam who was in a lot of great Westerns. There was a sensibility—my dad had a hand in showing me the good stuff.

M: It's interesting, because even though there's this age difference between Nick and me, it's never made a difference in terms of cultural references. I, too, watched *Taxi* and Jackie Gleason. I wouldn't think that Nick would know about Jackie Gleason, but he does. We like the same music, the same movies. I guess your friends in college exposed you to bands that you'd—

N: TOTALLY. That I'd missed. I flipped out on Pink Floyd only in my late twenties, when I lived with Pat Roberts. *(Awed voice)* "Holy shit! This band is fucking amazing!"
Also, in the early '90s, I was turned on to a band called the Beatles. It's a British band . . .

M: *(Laughs)*

N: I thought, "Oh my god!" It's hilarious.
But I want to say, in contrast to this "take your daughter to New York" sensibility . . . One thing I will say for my parents is that they did an amazing job . . . We had a Suburban, and my parents would pack all six of us in the Suburban, and we'd drive thirteen hours north every summer to go fishing in Minnesota. The whole

thing was very low-rent, but it was just the funnest family time together. We also took trips to the Black Hills, the Badlands, and Yellowstone. Just driving. And those were incredible.

One of the reasons the *Little House on the Prairie* books moved me so much is because of the many moments that remind me of my parents symbolically. For example, the kids always get gifts that they need—mother would get a half pound of sugar for Christmas, and the kids would always get, say, a sewing needle and three fishhooks. I hadn't thought about this for a long time, but my mother used to do the most intense treasure hunts for our birthdays. You'd come down to breakfast, and you'd get a note that was a clue that you had to figure out. She was so good at it—it would be a riddle you'd have to figure out.

Both my mom and dad used to write poems for special occasions. I remember for my grandparents' fiftieth anniversary, there was a big to-do at the American Legion Auxiliary in town. We put on a show that reenacted their life story together. My parents made a two-dimensional Model T Ford, and we all played our grandma and grandpa at different ages. My parents wrote the script—it was hilarious, and it rhymed! This is where I get my love for the simple A/B rhyme—really heartfelt with a few jokes.

M: My father was very funny, although very dark. And my mom is really funny. She continues—from the hospital bed in her living room, where she has twenty-four-hour care from some pretty extraordinary women—to lay us out from time to time. But my father was funny in a more outrageous, darker way. Occasionally we had family vacations. Once, when I was about eight, we went to Santa Fe. Back then it was tiny—really just the town square and a few streets off the square. A couple of hotels and restaurants. You'd drive out on dirt roads and there were cool little adobe houses. My parents had rented a house from some friends, and one day my father wanted to buy a piece of art, so we drove out to this art gallery. They left me in the car, which sounds really weird now that I'm saying it, but in the short time that my parents were inside the gallery, I met a boy named Pedro in the dirt parking lot and we fell deeply in love. We sat on the back of the car together and communed with each other's inner natures, mainly because I didn't speak Spanish and he didn't speak English. But we completely fell in love, to the point where we needed to be tearfully separated. I guess he was the son of the gallery owner? I don't know. But I do know that the love was such that he ran barefoot down the dirt road after our car for as long as he could, until we were out of sight. I had my tiny little hand pressed against the rear window of the car, tears streaming down my face, his little figure receding into the distance, never to be seen again.

N: *(Quietly)* You seem really wistful.

M: He was the one. *(Laughs)* My life could have been so different.

But I just want to tell you a story about Nick's family. Nick's mom was a labor-and-delivery nurse, and I thought, "That seems like a cute job, where she wraps babies up in little blankies and puts them in their little beddies."

She was getting ready to retire—this was recently—and Nick and I decided to drop in and see her at the hospital. And his mom, who is very quiet and self-effacing, comes out like freaking Rambo. There was nothing about his mom that heretofore would have led us to believe this was going to happen. But she comes tearing out in full . . . What's it called?

N: Scrubs.

M: With her hands up in the air, with gloves on, and she's like a whole other person, saying, "I don't have long to talk, I'm going in—there's a breech birth." So she goes in there, and delivers a baby by C-section. And that was my favorite, seeing Cathy in action. It was incredible.

And Nick's dad is very sweet. Even though I'm, like, two years younger than them, Nick's dad always puts his arm around me, says, (Ric voice) "You're getting pretty skinny there, kid! Better eat a potato." He treats me like a nineteen-year-old who he needs to make sure is eating.

N: He likes to make people a sandwich.

M: He's really sweet.

N: Sigh.

M: Is that it? Have we covered it, for crying out loud?

N: I think we've covered it.

(They Laugh)

M: High five!

N: High five! Peace out.

My Life as a Stripper

BY MEGAN

Part One

BEFORE I EVER SANG IN PUBLIC, I SANG A LOT *NOT* IN PUB-lic. Alone in the house, I sang like a mofo. That was from the time I was very little onward. I guess by the time I was old enough to be left alone in the house without a babysitter, that was when all bets were off, and shit would go down the second my parents were gone.

Like I've said, my parents somewhat mysteriously had a ton of Barbra Streisand and Judy Garland records. I would put on a record, and I would pick a song that I liked, and I would sing that song over and over again until I could sing it exactly like the record.

I had been singing just by myself, but then in about eleventh grade I joined the choir at my school, a fancy private school called Casady. The musical theater directors were a married couple named Mr. and Mrs. Fleming, and one day they said,

"Hey, you seem like you have a pretty good voice." They had some classical music that they wanted me to sing. They sent me to a voice teacher. She told me I was a coloratura soprano, which is hilarious. I guess I could probably do that with my voice, but my personality is about as far away from a coloratura soprano as it is from a person who could think of the perfect analogy to finish this sentence.

Eventually the Flemings had me get up in front of a few students and sing this classical piece, "Voi Che Sapete." I was absolutely beside myself with embarrassment and did a pretty horrible job.

The Flemings immediately dropped the coloratura soprano tack after that. I told them I really liked to sing musicals, that I liked to sing loud, big, belty show tunes. I don't know exactly how it went down, but I somehow ended up singing some show tunes for them. And they were like, "What?! You're going to do this in chapel in front of the entire school."

And I said, *faints*.

And they said, "Get up."

We had chapel every morning at my school. Every day at eight in the morning, you had to show up in chapel for thirty minutes. It wasn't religious. I don't really know what it was. It was kind of like a pep rally or something. We did sing a hymn or two, but I don't remember much religion being brought into it. I do remember when I was in lower school they read *The Lion, the Witch and the Wardrobe* to us. So I don't know what chapel was, exactly. But we had to go there every morning. I do know that.

So this one morning, February of my senior year, was the day of my performance. I was so nervous I didn't sleep for two nights before. I was a complete basket case. Because to get up in front of grades nine through twelve, every single person in those grades, and all of a sudden belt out three show tunes was insane.

Here was the set list: I thought I would start with something light, so "Don't Rain on My Parade" from *Funny Girl*, literally a cliché of the hardest possible song imaginable to sing. Second: "People," also from *Funny Girl*, and just the main song that had made people think that Barbra Streisand was the greatest singer who ever lived. *And* thirdly, for the big finish, fully choreographed by me in the style of Bob Fosse: "Razzle Dazzle" from *Chicago*.

So I got out there in front of everyone. Visual aid: I was wearing black pants with a black vest and a white turtleneck. That was the outfit. Very mime-esque, mime-era fashion. Mr. Fleming was my accompanist. We launched into "Don't Rain on My Parade"—again, a completely ridiculous song to pick for your first time singing in public in front of your entire school. I sang it, and held the long note at the end, and then it was over. There was a split second when I thought, "And suicide it is." And then everybody started screaming and cheering and stood up. They started throwing their knit hats and gloves up in the air. Everything was flying, and people were screaming, and I thought, "OMG."

I did "People" and got a similar reaction. And then I did "Razzle Dazzle." I had choreographed a point in the song where I literally went over and sat down on the principal's lap. This was pre–lap dancing, but I'm pretty sure I lap danced the principal. We were up in the altar area, in front of an Episcopal altar. The principal and vice principal were seated on either side in fancy carved booths. In spite of the religion-lite daily content, this was a full chapel with stained glass windows and choir stalls, and I went over and sat on the principal's lap while I was singing and did sexy moves.

So that was my first time singing in public. Afterward, everybody was way nicer to me than normal. Everybody thought I was hot shit for a while, even though I was still the same boring dude.

Part Two

As I may have mentioned, my father had a dark sense of humor, among other dark characteristics. He could be very funny, but most of his humor was very eccentric. He was early meta.

One of the things he loved to do, from the time I was quite young, say, first grade on, was to pretend he was having a massive heart attack and then "die" at the dinner table with his face in a plate of food. He couldn't be revived until it just got too hard to breathe in the spaghetti or whatever. The first few times it happened, my mother and I were like, "Wait . . . is he dead?" And after that, it was more like, *forced laugh*.

Another thing that he did—and I know for a fact that he was doing this when I was in third grade, because that was the only year I took the bus—I got off the bus one day and opened the front door. He was at the top of the stairs. I hated being alone with him because I was scared of him, so I said, "Where's Mommy?" And he said with this very grandiose vocal affectation he liked to use, "My darling, I'm sorry to tell you that your mother is dead." I was nine. At this point, I already pretty much knew that he was fucking with me, but for maybe five seconds, my heart shot out of my chest. Then I realized. "Wait. Where is she really, though?" And he said, "She's dead, my precious, I'm sorry. There was nothing we could do. You'll just have to live the rest of your life without a mother." And I said, "WHERE IS SHE?" And he said, "The grocery store."

So that was the kind of thing he did on an everyday basis. But it was either that or he was screaming at us, throwing something, smashing his fists down on the dinner table, or throwing a rolled-up newspaper at our toy poodle, who ended up having brain damage and walking backward. My grandmother eventually took him and he lived to be twenty-one.

Getting off the bus another fateful day in third grade, there was a little bit of a windfall—someone had thrown a giant stack of 45s onto our front yard, apparently out of the window of a car. I collected all of them, and there were some really good ones in there. One was especially great. The A-side was "Ebb Tide" and the B-side was "The Stripper." This started a whole stripping career for me, where I thought, "Well, I guess I'm going to be a stripper." I thought I was amazing at it. I played that record over and over. I had a pink feather boa that my mom had bought me—not because of my stripping career, just because I was a little girl and it was a pink feather boa. I had one of those little mirrors you get at the drugstore and stand up against the wall. A lot of my world took place in front of that mirror, and a lot of my future was foretold in front of that mirror. Not the stripping part, just making up songs and dances, performing. Once I had perfected one of my musical creations, I would then show it to my mom. But not the strip numbers. Those I would work on privately.

When I was a little older, about sixth grade, I had this friend from my ballet class named Nelly Goeke who would spend the night occasionally. At this point, I had two feather boas, both hot pink. I still had that stripper record, and she and I unearthed it.

We were in full stripping mode one day, and my mom walked in. And that was the last time Nelly Goeke got to come over to my house. The end of a beautiful friendship, and the end of what could have been a fabulous stripping duo, famed the world over.

Epilogue: I also had a friend down the street named DeeDee Fox. She wanted to be a Playboy Bunny. I wanted to be a stripper, and she wanted to be a Playboy Bunny. Maybe it was the music-and-dance aspect that drew me to stripping, because I remember being a little judgmental of DeeDee. "Playboy Bunny?! That's a lowly occupation. It's no stripping, but I guess it pays the bills." This aesthetic divide created a rift between us, and we eventually drifted apart—my first parting on grounds of creative differences.

CHAPTER 3

I Came Out Of The Womb In A Top Hat And Tap Shoes

Megan: *(To Nick)* When was it you realized that you were an artiste?

Nick: That's a good question. Maybe it was when my friends in college opened my eyes to the fact that I could do something as a creative person that could reach people. Up to that point, I realized I had a penchant for performing and knew I wanted to be in plays. I definitely had the passion to DO it, but in the first steps of adulthood, the steps to maturity—I think I've achieved about seventeen of the fifty-one so far—I realized that

I wanted to be an artist, and I wanted to make a difference with the stuff that I made in my life.

What about you?

M: *(Laughs)* I was very quiet and shy as a child. I was really introverted, and I never said much of anything. But when I was three—this is one of my super vivid memories—I was at my grandparents' house in Newport Beach. I was upstairs, and my grandparents, a couple of their friends, my uncle Taylor and aunt Jane, and my mother and father were in the living room. And I just remember thinking, "It's time." And then I thought, "But I can't go down with my hair looking like this." I was a big fan of Bozo the Clown at the time, although I was also deathly afraid of clowns, so I'm not sure what that means. There was a round banister on the stairs. I wrapped my hair around it to try to give it a curl. I held it for maybe ten seconds, thinking that would do the trick, and then let it go. It just flopped back down, and I thought, "This will have to do."

I raced downstairs, stood in the middle of what I now realize was a proscenium arch separating the dining room from two or three shallow steps down to the living room. I flung my arms out and yelled, "Ladies and gentlemen, introducing the World's Greatest Clown!" Then I proceeded to go into my act, which I hadn't planned out in any way, shape, or form, so it petered out pretty instantaneously.

N: It might be said that that was your act, in hindsight.

M: *(Laughs)* Right. I think the main event was that I was not only speaking, but doing something really uninhibited for the first time. But it wasn't like, from then on, Pandora's box had been opened. I went right back into my shell and didn't say anything else until I was, like, twenty-five.

N: But between your mom and your dad—you were born in LA, your dad was an actor. They were aware of, and in touch with, the arts. Your mom encouraged your dancing, she took you to New York.

M: Well, compared to your upbringing, for sure. But I feel like I got most of my jazz from TV. From the television.

N: You mean figurative jazz? Because I would like to know what program had all this jazz.

M: I was so in love with *Felix the Cat*, which was this really old cartoon that was super rad.

N: Yeah, me, too.

M: It was on when I was, like, three or four years old. I don't know if that would be enough to send me down the stairs to announce that I was the world's greatest clown, though. I don't know where I got that from, quite frankly. But I had it. Also, my first sentence was "Isn't this splendid?" And I apparently spoke in Italian when I was a baby. So . . . *(Laughs)* . . . I'm probably suffering from some undiagnosed brain disorder.

N: My first sentence was "Is there beer?"

M: *(Laughs)*

N: That's just a guess, though.

M: What was your second sentence? What was the response?

N: The response was in the affirmative, and my second sentence was "Yes, please. Just the one."

M: *(Laughs)* Just the one.

N: I don't have anywhere near the crazy, photographic memories that you have . . .

M: I remember being baptized when I was eighteen weeks old!

N: Also, you remember lengthy dreams with great alacrity. But one of the few things I do remember was when I was maybe four or five. My dad would have a card game, and they'd have a big case of twenty-four brown bottles of Alpine or Falstaff beer. My job was to keep everybody's cold beer refreshed. Then I would take the empties and put them in the return crate, under the coats, in the mudroom. And I would sit under the coats—it was really cold and dark under there among the work boots—and I would meticulously drain all the dregs from the beer bottles.

(Both laugh)

M: How old were you?

N: Four or five.

(More laughter)

N: Which could be considered an art. *(Clears throat)*

M: They say to be really accomplished at something, you need ten thousand hours of practice, so I guess . . . that would be . . .

N: It's one of my areas of mastery.

When I think about art in my life—I could go to a museum, I could go to a ballet, which I did every once in a while—I could go and appreciate the work and whatnot . . .

M: When did you go to ballets . . . ?

N: Well, I dated that ballet dancer for years.

M: Oh Christ on a cracker . . .

N: I don't know how to quantify it, but Joe Foust, my bosom friend, college roommate, and collaborator from the Defiant Theatre—I had friends as a kid who would turn me on to comic books, or music, but it wasn't my jam. Joe Foust was the first person who I thought, "Holy shit, you have all the right stuff. You have art and music and books and movies that are so delicious in a way I never knew." There were others—the next big one was Pat Roberts—and then you.

I pay a lot more attention to working. Left to my own devices, I'll say, "I'm going to go build something, or do some work."

M: All I ever want to do is read. I only leave the house under duress.

N: The breadth and number of books you read is jaw-dropping.

M: Thank you, I think. I've always been a big reader. When I was a kid, I would beg my mom to take me to the library, and I would check out, like, eleven books and read them all. From the time I was eight or nine, I always wanted to go to the library. I'd lie on the floor in my bedroom and read every single book.

N: Books were a big deal in our house. And that was where, more than anywhere else, my own creative voice and tastes began to develop.

M: I feel like reading was my acting class, like that was where I learned. Because most of the line when I read, I make the movie of the book in my head.

N: I'm going to blow this open a little bit . . .

M: *(Laughs)*

N: . . . and say in hindsight, and maybe I'm getting a little Wendell Berry, that because we didn't have art around my house, per se—there was Norman Rockwell, there was my father's Currier and Ives calendars—there wasn't art. But I feel like, much more than the classical definition of art, there was the art of the family, and the art of a low-income household. The art of living. *(Laughs)*

M: Caretaking.

N: I feel like it's still demonstrable in me.

M: Very much so.

N: I feel like I don't need to use the kitchen, because we live a luxurious life, but I'm driven to.

M: Not me! *(Laughs)*

I think that's true. And I didn't have those wholesome comforts of home so much. But my mom had a penchant for interior design, and that's something I think I inherited from her. She was pretty passionate about it, but her own '60s/'70s Jackie O version of it. I had that, and television, and movies sometimes. And music. But I didn't have the personal touch. You know. Of humans.

I already said this, but in the last few years, I've taken to saying that I came out of the womb in a top hat and tap shoes, because I think it's really interesting that from my earliest memory, I always wanted to do something creative. I used to draw—I still draw—

N: You're really good at drawing.

M: Thanks, honey! *(Both laugh)*

But the main thing for me, from the beginning, was music. Again, because I felt I could express myself emotionally or feel feelings I wasn't really allowed to display in real life.

I was in the car with my mom a lot. Where I grew up, everything is close together. If you were in the car for more than ten minutes, it was an outrageously long drive. So I don't know when these millions of hours I remember being in the car actually transpired, but that's how I remember it. And somehow, in these few minutes in the car, I managed to learn all the lyrics to every song on the radio, and sing it exactly along with whoever was singing it, male or female. And I'd be completely outraged if it wasn't in the right key for me and I'd have to transpose.

There was only one station that played "modern music." It was called WKY. And because it was basically the only game in town, they played everything. They played everything from the Stones to Frank Sinatra, and everything in between. I think it had a huge influence on me, because both of the bands I've had as an adult have been cover bands that run this crazy gamut of music from all different genres and eras.

N: Your bands are like a really eclectic, weird radio station art project.

It's interesting, now that I'm thinking about it—it's making more sense to me that I'm not a refined artist. My parents' art was taking three acres of land and drawing—"OK, this third of an acre will be a garden." They were both good at sketching out ideas. My dad designed a small barn, and he and I built it. I remember them building a three-bin compost corral out in the garden. And also this two-story decrepit farmhouse that we got for free. That was a work of art. And they figured out how to use four kids and their humble resources. Every other summer we would scrape and paint the entire wooden-sided house. I think they really instilled a sense of creativity in me, but one of great economy. They wouldn't go out and buy a set of paints. They would say, "What do we have here that we can do with?"

M: You have a good business sense, too. I wonder where that comes from?

N: It must inevitably come from them, as they, of course, are incredible keepers of a budget, raising four kids, most of the time, on a schoolteacher's salary. Because mom didn't go back to school until Matt was going to school on the bus.

M: Matt Damon.

N: Matt Damon, childhood friend and lodger.

(Both laugh)

M: He's the child you took in.

N: Yes, he went back to his family in, I believe, a South Boston neighborhood. He's never forgiven me.

M: I hope Affleck doesn't catch wind of this.

N: But talk about the nuts and bolts. I think both of us, once we hit *Will & Grace* and *Parks & Rec*, our career trajectories are pretty public knowledge. But I love all that stuff about *Risky Business* and *Blue Velvet*, and getting flown out from Chicago to LA because you were a foxy twentysomething wunderkind . . .

M: Basically, my deal was that I had the door shut to my only-child bedroom for most of my childhood coming up with magical moments, and I was in a ballet company. But I also did summer stock from the time I was twelve. There was a summer stock company in Oklahoma City called the Lyric Theatre. My father had done some shows there.

When I was twelve, I auditioned for *Fiddler on the Roof.* My mom and I decided I should sing "Do-Re-Mi," you know, "Do, a deer, a female deer" from *The Sound of Music*—I think that was the first movie I ever saw—as my audition. When I sang it for my mom and my father, they were like, "Uh-oh."

N: I'd love to hear you sing that song. And I'll be the children.

M: *(Laughs)* I'll sing it for you later.

N: *(Singing)* "Mi, a name I call myself. Fa, a long, long way to run.

M: Sing it!

N: Go on.

M: So. I did that show when I was twelve. Then I did a couple of shows there when I was fourteen. I was in the chorus, singing and dancing. I did *Kismet* and then *The Music Man.* I had super long hair, and I remember in *Kismet* there was a number where I had to whip my ponytail around in circles, and that was pretty scandalous. And when I was eighteen, I did *Shenandoah,* and that was my first real speaking part. But before that, also when I was eighteen, I got this weird summer job with these two guys from Oklahoma City—it was a random sequence of events. We somehow got booked at a club in Westwood, California, called Yesterdays, which at the time, in 1977, was the hottest game in town.

N: What was the name of the manager?

M: The manager of Yesterdays was named Brick Houston, and he was a former actor. I sang there—I was the entertainment, along with this guy who played guitar. I did that for the whole summer, and then I went back home and did *Shenandoah*.

I always say that I never had a job that was outside entertaining, but I did, kind of, because I taught ballet classes when I was in the ballet company.

N: But that doesn't count.

M: I taught ballet classes to children. *(Laughs)*

N: That was your flipping burgers.

M: I actually got the opportunity to choreograph a ballet, but I never did, because I ended up bowing out of the ballet company because I wanted to do other things. But I guess my love of making up dances for myself in my room has now carried over to me choreographing for Nancy And Beth.

Originally I wasn't going to go to college—I was just going to go to New York and audition for Broadway shows. Then my mom said, "I'll make a deal with you. Apply to one college, and if you get in, you'll go, and if you don't, you can go to New York." We decided on Northwestern, and I remember lying on the floor of my bedroom at two in the morning and writing the most bullshit essay in the history of the world for my college application. And then I somehow got accepted. So . . . hilarious.

N: So you were legitimately trying to throw the essay?

M: Yes! It was like *The Producers.*

N: Northwestern is going to be so pissed when they read this book . . .

M: Maybe they have a copy of it.

But I ended up going, and it was great. I tried to be a theater major at the beginning of my freshman year, but I was too freaked out because everyone was so uninhibited. I had never been around "theater kids" because I was the only person my age that I knew of in Oklahoma City who really had those kinds of aspirations, kind of like my father driving around in a Rolls-Royce wearing a cravat. I bought vintage clothes in high school, and wore my hair in a weird way. But I was the only one.

So I transferred out of the theater department almost immediately, into the Department of Interpretation, which is hilariously irrelevant and sounds very Kafkaesque to me now, but I did it because the chairman of that department was Frank Galati, who was a brilliant theater director. Interp, my major—which can't possibly still exist, right?—was the oral interpretation of prose, poetry, and theater. I'm not sure what the practical application of that is, but I did it, and it was fine, and then I basically just studied English and art history.

N: So what year was that?

M: That was 1978 and 1979.

N: So I'd just like to throw in . . .

M: That you were nine?

N: I'd like to throw in a nugget. In 1994, Frank Galati cast me in the adaptation of *As I Lay Dying* at Steppenwolf, and I believe it was the only time in my life that I was cast as the hunk.

M: Wait, do you want to hear something even crazier? I auditioned for that.

N: WHAT?

M: Yeah. I didn't get it.

N: I was the hunk to the character you would have played. Her name was Dewey Dell.

M: Oh, wait. No, it was something else. I think it was *A Death in the Family* by James Agee. *(Laughs)* It would have been weird if we were both in the same show and didn't realize it until just now.

N: That would have gotten this started way sooner.

M: *(Laughs)* So at Northwestern, even though I wasn't a theater major, when I was a freshman they were going to do *A Little Night Music*, which is a Sondheim musical. I decided I would audition for it, and everyone said, "Don't even bother because freshmen never get cast in University Theatre productions." So I thought . . .

N: *(Funny voice)* Guess what happened . . .

M: I thought, Well then why didn't I just move to New York? So I auditioned and got cast as the maid, Petra, who has this song called "The Miller's Son." Everybody was furious. But that production was when I realized that I didn't know anything about acting. I had a little acting experience from those summer stock productions I did in Oklahoma City, but very minimal. However, this girl who was a sophomore, who was also in the show, was incredible. Her name was Suzie Plakson. She met up with me at my dorm, and I said, "I don't get it." And she said, "You know your character in the show? Make friends with her." I said, "What do you mean?" and she just repeated, "Make friends with her." And that was a turning point because, ultimately, that somehow made sense to me. Also, a few years later, I was supposed to do a part in a movie that was pretty bad, where I had to get drunk and barf and then make out with a guy in the scene. I was with Laurie Metcalf and John Malkovich at a flea market in Pasadena, and I was supposed to shoot it the next day. I said, "Laurie, I don't know how I'm going to do this part. It's horrible." I described the role to her, and she said, "Make her really happy." And I did. And it worked . . . and it's been working ever since. *(Laughs)* And that is my career trajectory. Thanks, everybody!

N: Good-bye!

What is it about our career trajectories that is applicable to our relationship? The headline is that even though we both come with very different skill sets and are years apart, and from Oklahoma and Minooka, pretty disparate locations, we hit a lot of the same touchstones on the way. The main one being with the Steppenwolf people in Chicago.

I think it's interesting that we both kind of went our way until our late thirties, when we had the uncanny, incredibly unlikely experience that we both got our jobs on our TV shows, popular Thursday night shows.

M: How old were you?

N: Thirty-eight.

M: And I was thirty-nine. And what are the chances that the only two members of the same household would both get jobs on half-hour network comedies that became popular shows? And both of our characters became—I don't want to say became iconic, but more or less became fairly iconic characters. What are the chances of that happening?

N: I think that can be said without sounding like backpatting. I think it's pretty factual that they were both unique standouts in their own way. And not only that, but both NBC, both Thursday night, both shot on the same lot. It's really nutty. And something that we've touched on in other chapters—it's really interesting because *Will & Grace* was a bigger ratings hit. You did, what, two hundred episodes?

M: One hundred ninety-four. Now 210, I think . . . ?

N: We did 125. *Will & Grace* won a bunch of Emmys. Megan got nominated seven times and won twice, I believe?

M: C'mon, Bob.

N: Plus scads of other awards. *Parks & Rec* was left very much alone *(Laughs)* by the award shows, by and large. We got a couple of nominations here and there, but very few.

M: *(Whispers)* You got a Critics' Choice Award.

N: Regardless of my participation, it was a very different experience. Our show also came about . . . There was the transition between the majority of people watching on broadcast to the majority of young people, especially, watching on their computers. And that was something our show had to deal with, because our ratings were much lower, because they weren't yet counting the ratings of people watching on other broadcast services, or streaming, or whatever.

In any case, they had a similar impact in terms of taking our careers several notches higher, to a level where people suddenly knew who we were. We came out of the situation with a clout that we didn't have previously.

M: I think the great thing about being able to achieve a degree of success like that is that it just opens doors. It opens other doors that you hadn't been able to unlock before. That's the best thing about it.

N: I agree. Moving to LA from Chicago—that was the theater kid's dream, at least to me. If I could get on some show, like David Schwimmer, who had left Chicago theater and got on *Friends* and made a bundle, then you could afford to make whatever artistic choices you wanted to. Because your rent has been paid, with plenty left over for making art, if you're not stupid.

It brings to mind when, about fifteen years ago, I was attached to a great, weird little indie comedy with some guys who had been attached to Steven Soderbergh over the years. They were part of his team. At the same time we were trying to get that movie green-lit, Steven was also trying to get a movie adaptation of the great comedy novel *Confederacy of Dunces* off the ground. Will Ferrell was supposed to play Ignatius at the time. It's legendary: John Belushi, John Candy, Will Ferrell, Zach Galifianakis—at one point, Vince Vaughn was mentioned. All these different comedy guys were supposed to play this incredibly plum role at different points. And I remember thinking, "God, I wonder what would have to happen for that part to come around to me someday?"

Amazingly, about twelve years later, it was Steven Soderbergh's longtime collaborator John Hardy and independent producer Bob Guza who eventually hired me to star in a stage production of *Confederacy*, in the role I had so passionately craved. Mr. Soderbergh even came on as an additional producer. The show was a big hit, and impossibly fun, which just goes to show that you never know what little offshoot of the path will lead to further satisfaction. I found that very moving. When we were first doing a script workshop reading in New York, at intermission we were peeing next to each other, and I said, "Hey, John, this is going great, thank you again for having me. But I just have to ask you, how did you ever think of me? How did you think I could do this?" Because everyone thinks of me as some sort of manly, sheriff–Ron Swanson type. And he said, "I don't know. We just had this feeling."

I found it kind of strange, especially since the guy had known me for a long time. And humorously, when we were going into production with the play and I was going back and forth with the director about what kind of mustache we should do for Ignatius, if we should do something real or prosthetic and whatnot, and I did a Google image search of Ignatius, the seventh thing that came up was Ron Swanson from an episode where Ron was sick. He had a hunting cap on, like Ignatius, and scarves, and I was at my chubbiest, and constricting my face so I had several chins—which is one of the cool looks I do—

M: Hold me back.

N: —and it looked just like Ignatius. And I thought, "Aha. Maybe the producers didn't just think of me out of the blue as much as I think they looked at this photo and said, 'This is our guy.'"

But that's the kind of thing that a job like *Parks & Rec*, or *Will & Grace*, will do for you. Makes people think, "He could be the person."

M: On the subject of synchronicity, I have had some crazy things happen. The first time my parents took me to see a Broadway musical, I was sixteen. It was *Chicago* with Gwen Verdon and Chita Rivera. And then years later, the first big successful job I ever got was a Broadway revival of the musical *How to Succeed in Business Without Really Trying* with Matthew Broderick. And it was at that same theater where I'd seen *Chicago* when I was sixteen.

Then, the first Broadway play my parents took me to see was *Equus*, also when I was sixteen, and that was at the Plymouth Theatre, now poetically renamed the Schoenfeld, and I recently did my first Broadway play, Terrence McNally's *It's Only a Play*, at that same theater with Nathan Lane and, again, Matthew Broderick.

When I was about fifteen, the first taping of a sitcom I saw was *The Bob Newhart Show*, when we were in Los Angeles on vacation. Years later, we filmed the first eight seasons of *Will & Grace* on that same soundstage on the CBS Radford lot. That's pretty crazy.

N: Yes, it's uncanny.

M: You're uncanny.

N: Also, it seems on topic that once you and I started having sex, you started winning acting awards, like, hand over fist.

M: Hand over fist would apply to our sex lives as well.

N: There's a lot of synchronicity.

M: A lot of magical realism.
I wanted to add that if we're going to isolate my few acting lessons, there's the one with Suzie Plakson, and the one with Laurie Metcalf, but the first one was actually when I was doing that production of *Fiddler on the Roof* in Oklahoma City when I was twelve. Another little girl and I were playing the two youngest of the five daughters. My character's name was Shprintze, and her character's name was Bielke, I believe.

N: Shprintze's the better of . . .

M: Shprintze's the fox. I guess we really were murdering the dialogue. It was bad. We only had probably three or four lines apiece. We were rehearsing one day in this big ballet studio.

N: Which is where they shot *I Love Lucy*, crazily.

M: *(Laughs)* Can you believe?

N: It all ties together.

M: The whole cast was in this ballet studio, and the director said, "Everybody sit down against the wall." The whole cast sat down. He said, "Megan"—and the little girl who was playing my sister, I can't remember her name—"come right out here to the middle of the room and sit down on the floor." We did, and he turned off all the lights. It was pitch-black in this windowless room. And I'm sure most of the cast started making out and groping each other, because that was really happening in that show. I learned a lot. And he said, "Now, say your lines!"

There was a line where we were supposed to jump up and down, and say, "We're going on a train and a boat. We're going on a train and a boat." And he made us say it in the pitch-dark. And for some reason, à la Helen Keller, it kind of clicked, that we were saying an actual sentence, in English: "We're going on a train and a boat." And it all suddenly made sense to me. They're just normal words that a person would say.

N: Were you possibly, as a kid, distracted?

M: *(Laughs)* Was I distracted? You didn't know who the Beatles were till you were in college. *(Both laugh)* I think because we were kids, we were just going through the motions without it having any meaning. We didn't understand that you just had to make it real. It's language, and you can utter it so it seems like it comes from an actual human on the planet.

It's just funny how things sort of flow along, how one thing leads to the next. For me, my big break was doing *How to Succeed in Business* when I was thirty-five, after I'd already been kicking around Los Angeles for nine years. We were doing the show out of town at the La Jolla Playhouse, and we got a review in the *Hollywood Reporter.* The reviewer singled me out in a way that created a minor hysteria, and I got a new agent, and a lot of good things started happening. I'd always been lucky with that kind of stuff—I had been flown out for screen tests for movies when I was in Chicago doing theater, like the lead in *Risky Business* and things like that. I had agents from Los Angeles pursuing me when I still lived in this little apartment in Chicago just doing theater. I moved out to Los Angeles when I was twenty-six, and I got signed at William Morris within the first two weeks. I don't know—I just was lucky. I worked pretty steadily. There were a couple times my parents had to help me pay my rent, but other than that, I did pretty well. I'd book a pilot pretty much every year, but they usually didn't go. *(Laughs)* They'd go for seven episodes, or thirteen, or zero. And that was that.

But I think a really key element in all of this is that maybe neither one of us was ready until we were a little older for any kind of appreciable success. I had a lot of talents, but I didn't have a lot of skills in the real-life department, in terms of human interactions. And I'm not talking about the workplace, I'm talking about relationships. So if I'd gotten the lead in *Risky*

Business, or any of those other big jobs then, I don't think I would have been able to handle it very well. There might have been a bit of a Lindsay Lohan situation. I don't know. I think everything happens in the time and the way that it's supposed to happen.

SEX NINJA

BY NICK

LOOK, PEOPLE. I HAVE HEARD A LOT OF YOU OVER THE years brazenly claim to be Megan Mullally's biggest fan. In autograph lines, meet and greets, backstage greenrooms, grocery stores, lumber yards, airports, and just randomly out in public, you have run the gamut of humanity: from sweet-faced California Cub Scout to turnip-nosed Manhattan nun; from granite-jawed North Dakota big-rig trucker to pugnacious Skokie lipstick lesbian whose knifing stare would make either of the Hemsworth lads skulk silently to the valet stand, waggling his ticket with sheer panic. Each and every one of you has stared me defiantly in the eye and held forth that your fanaticism in the worship of my wife was easily greater, breezily more maniacal, than my own obsessed ardor of eighteen years and counting.

When I have, countless times over the years, apprehended such an affront, when you have said to me something to the effect of "I'm sorry, but your wife is the most amazing creature consuming oxygen, and so I am ready to entirely supplicate myself at her feet," always with the implied "I am ready to defeat you in a contest of Megan Mullally adoration," I have taken the high road, nodding and smiling affably, wearing my pacifism like an uncomfortable set of fake teeth, with a "Yes, sure, I agree!" Privately I am breathing deeply through my willfully unflared nostrils, maintaining my equanimity, because the answer I would prefer to serve to you pilgrims would be "No shit, Sherlock. I enjoy the flesh-and-blood version of her every day" and "If you love her so much, why don't you marry her? Oh, because I already did, so you can't marry her as she is unavailable because she picked *me*, you goddamn sneering little Cub Scout. Eighteen years ago. Eighteen and a half. So back your bad self up a step because you happen to be addressing Mr. Mullally right now. You think you're her fan? I have taken a *vow for life* to have and to hold her, through good times and sick times and also shitty parts, something like that, and she has made the same promise to me, friend." The first thing I see every morning (when I am allowed to sleep in her chambers, usually at *least* second Tuesdays) is her sweet visage, very much like a freckly fawn/bunny/wood nymph/faerie queen, so you are welcome to "toss as many shades" as you like upon my lamp, neighbor, because I have most certainly won this paragraph. Motherfucker.

OK, that feels better. With that preamble out of the way, I would like to write a little something about what it's like to work as an actor with a person like my wife, if you also happen to be married to that person. I have often said that Megan is like if a person could be a Mel Brooks movie all in one tiny package, but even that statement, meant as a substantial compliment, feels lacking to me, partly because Mr. Brooks's films, however classic and genius, necessarily brandish a decidedly male point of view, and of the many descriptors that one can successfully apply to Megan Mullally, "male" is not one of them.

Of Megan's abilities and work ethic I have written at some length in my many (three) other books, but on this particular aspect I feel that I have to date not elaborated satisfactorily. As previously noted, we met working together in a stage play in Los Angeles, which is where and when many of the weapons in her arsenal were revealed to me. During the spring (of 2000) in which we became acquainted onstage, I also spent some time at the house of a friend who had a television (I then had for entertainment only a twelve-inch DeWalt Sliding Compound Miter Saw), and on that television I sweatily watched my first reruns of *Will & Grace*—hilarious episodes in which even more of her tool kit was on display.

What became immediately clear was that I was dealing with an artist who, if we had been competing in the Olympics, would have astonished one and all, year after year, with enough variety to her prowess that I guess she would have belonged in the decathlon. Her karate was on point, is what I'm trying to say. If an image of her clearing the pole vault bar was on the box of wheat flakes, I would probably still be eating breakfast cereal, is what I mean to get across. Not only did her comedy slay in two very distinct mediums (television situation comedy and stage play), but her dramatic acting was also poignantly sincere and effective. She also displayed a bit of delectable singing and dancing that spring, every bit of which seemed effortless and completely off-the-cuff but in reality had been artfully curated.

In the nearly nineteen years that I have stood at her side, I have never once seen Megan "phone in" an effort. She will stay up way too late the night before a performance, perfecting her schtick/song/dialogue/dialect until she is satisfied that she's ready to make the kill. Because that's what she is, really. She's like an artisanal assassin—the kind who meticulously lays out her weapons before even leaving the house on her deadly assignment, reassuring herself of the sharpness of the blades and devastating weight of the blunt cudgels so that she *does not miss.* You, her victim, never see it coming. In fact, you are probably thinking that you're having the time of your life, when suddenly—*snikt!*—you have been slain by my wife, the ninja.

As we embarked upon our life together, I got to witness firsthand the accuracy with which she laid out her victims on a weekly basis at the *Will & Grace* soundstage, never more so than when I had a small role as a plumber, and it was all I could do to escape with my skin intact. That show, even when I appeared on it back in 2001, was an incredibly well-oiled machine thanks to the mastery of director Jimmy Burrows, the whip-smart writers, and the top-drawer cast, not to mention the crew of champions behind the scenes. Which means for a Chicago theater kid performing on his first sitcom, everything was fast, sharp, and utterly terrifying. One good thing I learned then about working with Megan is that all one really has to do is stand still and recite the dialogue at the proper interval, and you're home free, because if Megan is in the picture, then nobody ever looks at you, for obvious reasons. At one point in the taping I stepped off course too far downstage, and there came an immediate, involuntary "ARGGHGHHHH" from the audience and the crew alike, which instructed me to immediately remove myself from their eye line to her. This is how we learn. It's a tough business.

Over the years we worked together in more plays with our Los Angeles theater company, called Evidence Room, and my education proceeded apace. We also appeared in some independent films together, but never really facing off or getting to work as a team. So in 2009, when Mike Schur (*Parks and Recreation* creator) came to me and said, "We have devised this ex-wife character who is a raging bitch, works at the library, and has an evil sexual hold over Ron Swanson"—my character—"whom she can make do the most insane things with her spell-binding sexuality . . . Do you think Megan would want to play her?" I felt something very special happening in my lower-belly region. When I described the offer to Megan, she simply replied, "Tell them yes, but I want to take my top off." I expired and fell to the floor, neatly murdered once again by the Sex Ninja.

We ended up getting to do a handful of "Ron and Tammy" episodes, and they were nearly my undoing, as an artist and as a man. You see, now that I've given you some idea of Megan's acumen in the thespianic arts, as well as my slavish devotion to said acumen, you can then understand how I was the most helpless sitting duck for her techniques in dealing comedy death. When she made a "sex face" at me and then proceeded to slap herself on the cheek of that face with a large plank of beef jerky, what was I to do but perish? All of my fancy University of Illinois Shakespeare training could not have remotely prepared me for the onslaught of Megan Mullally–brand wiles of seduction. The sheer force of her carnal punches obliterated any professional resistance what-soever on my part, the type of resistance upon which I would normally rely in any given scene requiring me to look at a very funny person without cracking a smile. I have withstood Will Ferrell and Amy Poehler. I have tolerated Jason Sudeikis, Will Forte, and Andy Samberg. I have stoically endured soft-core porn scenarios with Eric McCormack and Debra Messing. Chris Pratt! The cast of *Childrens Hospital*! Melissa McCar-thy! Even Conan O'Brien, of whom it has been said, "To even countenance his puppet's physique is to chortle with gaiety!" All of these master clowns and more have I resisted, but I have never been, and Lord willing never will be, equipped to resist the love shuriken of my wife, the ninja of my heart.

CHAPTER 4

You're So Much Of A Whore

Nick: What's our topic?

Megan: It's a double. First topic: PAST RELATIONSHIPS!

> **N:** Should I just hand this to you?
>
> **M:** I resent your tone! *(Laughing)*
>
> **N:** *(Laughing)* I've also had some ...
>
> **M:** You've had, like, one! So this is going to be a short amount of talking from you ...
>
> **N:** I won't have to talk much because ... you're ... so much ...
>
> **M:** ... of a whore ...?

(Both laugh)

N: The difference here is that you were my first grown-up relationship. I had a couple of long-term relationships before ours, but I was still young to be heading toward marriage.

M: Sigh.

N: So why don't I get mine out of the way? The only one I had in my twenties that was of any length was with Cecilia. And it was only a couple of years, tops, if that. Looking back on it, it seems pretty collegiate. It was when I was living in that warehouse where you had to walk a quarter mile to use the bathroom. Or pee off the fire escape. We did *The Crucible* together, and it was a show romance that just lasted for a while. We were supposed to move to LA together, but she got cold feet and disappeared entirely. Turned up back in Mexico, where she was from, sometime later with her family.

M: Don't tell Trump.

N: My contribution feels pretty lightweight on this topic.

M: So this will just be my exclusive chapter.

N: You had previous relationships?

M: *(Laughs)* I had a boyfriend when I was four.

N: OK, that's one. Is that it?

M: Then I had a boyfriend in kindergarten.

N: Two.

M: Billy Tillman.

N: I met Billy Tillman.

M: You did. There's still a spark.

N: I let him keep his kneecaps. So far.

M: *(Laughs)* I had a boyfriend in first grade named Terry Traub. We kissed lying down in his driveway, and his sister saw us.

N: I haven't met that motherfucker.

M: I had a boyfriend in second grade named Mike Mee. Then I had a boyfriend in third grade named Chip Oppenheim.

(Both laugh)

M: Who is someone Nick knows quite well.

N: I've met that sonofabitch. Dangerous.

M: Then I had a boyfriend in fourth grade named Mike Mee. I went back to my second-grade love. We used to lie under his trampoline and kiss. When no one was jumping on it, mostly.

N: You mind if I step into the other room? Because this is going south real quick. . . .

M: *(Laughs)* It went on like that, really, up until the day I met you. And then I homed in. But yeah, I had a lot of boyfriendies, most of them extremely forgettable, and some of them only memorable because of their hideousness. I mean, in adult life. Kindergarten through fourth grade went pretty well. And I was definitely the shot-caller in those relationships.

N: You don't say.

M: On the playground, there was a bush . . . Let me finish . . .

N: *(Laughs)* What age was this?

M: You know, second grade. And it was hollow in the middle, and I would sit in there . . .

N: In Oklahoma City, if there's grass on the field, play ball.

M: I would sit in there, and I was the queen. All these boys who were my courtiers—I would send them out on errands to fetch me twigs and stones. To do my bidding in general. So it really just went on from there. Things never slowed.

N: Wow.

M: I was a very sexual child. I had a recurring dream from the time I was three that there was a witch who would put me in an oven and cook me, and then she would take me out and eat me. And when I was warming up in the oven, I would think, "Yeah. Fucking cook it, bitch."

N: And you later realized the witch resembled Pat Benatar.

M: No. It was just the idea of getting heated up in that oven.

N: Sure.

M: You're not springing a woody over there?

N: I'm getting pretty interested over here.

M: *(Laughs)* Maybe you should ask me questions? There's too much material.

N: I don't know if we're going to start with the whole litany . . . I was thinking major relationships.

M: I was, too, but mine were so much more serious than yours that I hesitate to launch into that.

N: So where did we leave off? You were the queen of the bush.

M: Queen of the bush. In high school, fortunately for you— I would probably be married with nine children if I hadn't been in that ballet company—I was too busy to have a full-time boyfriend, because I was rehearsing every night. So when I went away to college, that was my first actual grown-up boyfriend. I didn't know how to have a real boyfriend. He kind of wore me down until I finally said "I love you" back.

N: You don't seem worn down to me.

M: That's really nice. I'm just talking about my puss.

N: Me, too.

M: Amazing. Anyway, we were together for three and a half years. My first relationship was when I discovered I was completely insane. Let me rephrase that. My first relationship was when I discovered I was crazy. And I mean only when it came to relationships, because I'd never been in one before, and I didn't realize how my upbringing would manifest until I got into a relationship where it was applicable to be things like irrationally jealous, et cetera. Before that, nothing had surfaced, because I wasn't in a relationship. But then I realized I had these problems, and my boyfriend realized I had these problems. And we both became progressively less enthused. I tried to change, but didn't have the tools, and didn't understand anything about myself or how normal people were supposed to be in a relationship. I had absolutely no clue. But it was my first real sexual relationship, I guess.

N: The sound of a recording device hitting the wall.

M: *(Laughs)* But I have since realized that as much as I had problems that I didn't understand and didn't know how to deal with, he wasn't perfect either. I mean, no one is?

N: Who is? *(Pause)* Conan O'Brien.

M: Don Lemon.

So that was that. And then I had a kind of nice relationship with a guy in Chicago named Joe. That was a four-year-long thing. I wanted to move to New York and audition for Broadway musicals, and he wanted to go to Los Angeles, so he suggested we go to Los Angeles for a month, and then New York for a month. We came out to Los Angeles first. I had already been flown out here for those screen tests, so I already knew some agents and casting directors. So I got signed by an agency right away and never left. Joe was very close to his parents and didn't want to be away from them. He actually still lived at home. He was Italian.

N: Consequently, we like to give Italians a hard time. Fucking pasta all over the house.

M: A lot of pasta strewn everywhere. A lot of V8 juice. Wait, that's not Italian. *(Fake Italian accent)* "I wish I had a tomato! That's one-a spicy meat-a-ball-a!" He said that a lot.

N: *(Same accent)* "I wish I had a V8!"

M: *(Laughs)* He very unceremoniously moved back to Chicago two weeks after we moved to Los Angeles and just left me hanging on my own, when we were supposed to be renting an apartment together. I had just signed with William Morris and was getting a bunch of auditions and didn't want to leave. He kept going back and forth from Chicago to LA and that was kind of the end of that. But he was a nice guy. Next to Nick, he was the nicest person I'd dated.

Why don't we break this up? Let's get into your reminiscences.

N: I guess my first real girlfriend was in high school. She was a cheerleader. She was just exuberant. She played the flute. But we weren't really cut out—

M: "Played the flute"? Is that a euphemism?

N: It's not. Although we did also engage in physical affection. *(Laughs)*

M: I'm sure. I read your book.

N: *(Laughs)* That ended when I started dating another young lady, who was a born-again Christian, and I pretended to be a born-again Christian so we could date. That actually lasted for four years or so. But it wasn't very healthy, because there was some insincerity happening on both our parts.

That saw me into college. I had a lot of fun in college. I had one serious relationship with a woman who was a stage manager.

M: Read: lesbian.

N: She had some insecurity issues that she wasn't getting around. I really liked her a lot. But it ultimately drove us apart. I'm sure I was also not a complete picnic.

Then, in Chicago, I had a girlfriend who worked in the costume shop at the Goodman. She was pretty terrific—she could play They Might Be Giants songs on the guitar. But she said pretty immediately, "Let's get married and have kids." I was twenty-three, and she was twenty-eight. And I was . . . not quite there. And so we had an amicable parting. Then I had another girlfriend who worked as a costume designer at Steppenwolf. We had a very nice time, and she said, "Let's get married and have kids." And I said, "I'm not there."

M: See, if I had said that, you probably wouldn't have wanted to do it. I just never said it. I was like, "Let's NOT get married."

N: No, by the time I met you, I believe I was there. I was ready. With the others, it just wasn't yet a case of "I want to spend my life with you." I think part of it was that I knew inhcrently that I wouldn't be staying in Chicago? Then, there was the spicy interlude of one month with a heavy metal singer who had an EKG tattooed on the side of her head . . .

M: Didn't she throw you into the bathtub or something?

N: There was a bathtub incident.

M: Maybe don't relay that one. Leave it at "bathtub incident" and let people think about it.

N: It was a very tempestuous and illicit month of hijinks.

M: I had a tempestuous and illicit thirty-year period.

N: So I have some catching up to do. But because of the degree of felonious activity, after a month of it, I decided it was not the life path I needed to be pursuing. And that's about it. *(Laughs)* Back over to you.

M: I had a few . . . I'm just telling you the ones that were the most significant. Let's just say I always had some boyfriend or husband or something. But I didn't really have sexual intercourse with that many people. It just sounds like I did. Apparently, I have an amorous nature. And Nick has reaped the benefits. May I say that?

N: Sure.

M: And will you refute it?

N: No, you'll brook no disagreement from these quarters.

M: So the ones that stand out are the two that I mentioned. And some that stand out because they were hilariously bad. There's sort of an illicit one that might stand out a tad, which I will not talk about in book form.

N: Which one is that? Oh—you mean before he married Angelina Jolie? Between Jen and Angelina?
You know, I would add a nod—"to the other women I palled around with," a gesture of gratitude and respect for some very nice romantic times while we were all getting our feet under us. Because in my twenties, I made sure I didn't get into anything serious. I played it very fast and loose for a time. Because I knew I wasn't settled at all. I inherently knew I wasn't staying.

M: Yeah, as far as sex in general goes, if it's consensual and with a nice person and you're not breaking any laws, where's the bad part?

N: I can't wait to try it.

M: Maybe someday. We'll see.

N: OK, I'm here.

M: Just try to stay in a neutral space about it. I can't make any promises.

By the time I met Nick, I had not been in a serious relationship for four years, and I didn't want to be. I had mastered the art of the fling, and I was doing that intermittently. Then I met Nick, and Nick is just— He might as well be wearing a sign around his neck that says, "Not Fling Material." And I thought, "I can't get involved with this guy, because it will have to be a relationship." And that's why I held him off for a while. But I just liked him so much as a person. And then I fell in love with him.

I've known the musician Tom Waits and his wife, Kathleen Brennan, since 1985. She and Tom had already been together for several years when I met them. I said, "It seems like you guys have such a great relationship," and she said, "We've been together all these years, and it always feels like the first time." And that's kind of how I feel about Nick. Even though we've been together for eighteen years ...

N: *(Singing)* "I would climb any mountain, sail across the stormy sea ..."

M: *(Laughs)* It's nice to have a soundtrack.

I don't want to use the word "fresh," but it always feels new and fun and like we just got together. I just like him and what he has to say. I think he's funny. And nice. And that's a good thing, to not be sick of each other. Or super irritated by everything the other person does. That's the luckiest thing, because then you can be together forever. The problem with a lot of my exes—and I'm sure you feel the same, Nick—is that at a certain point, sometimes way sooner than one might've hoped, everything about them just makes you want to jump out of a moving vehicle. "I would rather jump out of this car that's going forty-five miles an hour than listen to one more millisecond of this person speaking."

N: Sure.

M: Unfortunately, because I didn't know what a normal relationship was supposed to be like, I'd just think, "Maybe it's my fault that this person is driving me to drink. Because this is a perfectly nice person on paper." I didn't understand that there are very few people that . . . You're very lucky if you find one person who you're actually compatible with. But if you do find that one person, odds are that you're going to stay together.

There was some fun palling around on my part also. And when you get older, you look back and think, "Oh, the rock drummer with the BO and the vintage plaid pants! He was awesome!"

N: I'm having a flood of memories. I had a juvenile idea that I should be able to be a player. It comes from growing up in a rural area and watching a lot of music videos. "Man, if shit goes right, I'm going to drive a Corvette like David Lee Roth. There'll be chicks in bikinis, and I'm going to be having tons of crazy casual sex." And I tried that, I tried having . . .

M: *(Laughs)* That's so not you.

N: I tried playing around. And I failed, because my parents' influence was so strong. "Look, I know we just did a bunch of drugs, and we're going to have sex, but I feel like we should have a meaningful relationship first." That was my problem.

There was one time, back when I knew I would be leaving Chicago. My girlfriend from *The Crucible*, Cecilia, had disappeared and I had six or eight months left. I was dating a couple of women who were great. If I had stayed in Chicago, one of them may have developed into something. But one of them—she was one of those—maybe once a year, we'd run into each other and hook up. She always had a boyfriend, and I never knew . . . it was always a different boyfriend. But it became a thing. She was brazen about having a thing for me, and she'd tell her boyfriend. It was the only time I was ever involved in something like that. I eventually had a rare moment of maturity where I said, "I don't want to indulge in this. I don't think that's right, what you're doing." It was interesting. That was kind of my own—I guess I grew up all of a sudden, to the point where I was done playing around.

Then things got pretty bleak. *(Laughs)* I moved to Los Angeles. I was maturing enough that I wanted to find something more serious. And man, I could not find a

lady. Every time my friend Pat and I would go anywhere and meet someone who was cool—because he
was also on the make—it became a rule that they were
either married or gay. It became laughable. As soon as
we'd meet someone who was cool, we'd say, "Are you
married?" And they'd say, "I'm a lesbian. And yes."

M: This might sound weird, but I think I always knew
that someday I'd find the right guy.
It's funny that I always assumed I'd eventually have a
happy relationship, because my parents had a terrible
relationship—and then, it happened.

N: Boom.

M: Papi, do I treat you right?

N: Yeah. I keep asking you to treat me more like the game-
keeper.

M: *(Laughs)* Nick just paused and said, "You're not going to talk about so-and-so? And so-and-so?" And I
said, "No." Because they don't factor in to this. I'm mentioning only the relationships that for whatever reason
were the most significant or had the most impact.

N: So those other ones would be included in the general
"mistake" comments that you made. Rather than
going into specifics.

M: Yes. The ones that I didn't mention would all be lumped
into "not as memorable," even if you'd think on paper
that they'd be more memorable.

N: I just remembered, actually—it's pretty juicy if I talk about my first girlfriend.

M: The flautist?

N: No, this was in junior high. She was a cheerleader—see a pattern here?

M: How many cheerleaders are there in Minooka?

N: There are, like, fifteen girls in the class, and twelve of them are cheerleaders. So the odds are in my favor. She was from the next school over, Channahon, where my dad taught.

M: Long-distance relationship!

N: Yeah. We met, and her friend somehow got my phone number, and called me and said, "Michelle likes you." And I said, "Where do I sign?" We talked on the phone and started going together before we met. *(Laughs)*

M: *(Incredulous)* Wow . . . That's like early Tinder or something.

N: We'd seen each other, but I don't think we'd shaken hands or anything. So we started this thing up, and . . . maybe we went to something once and held hands. I think it was the roller-skating rink. But we never kissed or anything. It was pretty brief. But the intrigue is that her name is Michelle McCoy, and years later, I found out that my dad had been adopted by my grandpa Offerman, and that he was a Hatfield by blood.

M: *(Laughs)* Oh my god! That's a real *Romeo and Juliet* situation right there.

N: So I guess it wasn't meant to be for this Hatfield and that McCoy.

M: That's dramatic!

I was going to say one other thing: I mysteriously attracted to myself a number of fully gay men who, for whatever reason, wanted to make out with me and have romantic relationships. So there were, like, four gay men who I had relationships with. Not having coitus, but other things. Very strange. Four gay men who made the first move, and I was like, "All right."

N: You don't count me among those?

M: I do. Indeed.

N: Am I the third or fourth?

M: You're the fifth. The fifth and final gay man.

N: I'm a growing concern.

M: *(Laughs)*

N: I'm developing some thoughts . . .

M: He is. He's still developing his gayness.

I don't know. I was never like Gisele Bündchen, but for some reason, I had suitors.

N: First of all, foul on the past-tense verb. I've seen photographs. From soup to nuts, you've been the foxiest thing in the county.

M: *(Laughs)*

N: The pictures of you, from ballet and high school—I would have crashed my car if I drove by you. You're being very modest.
I'm trying to remember if there's anything I left out.

M: Come on, who are you kidding? That's one of the really big reasons that I love you. Because you're not the kind of guy who had a million women and was a dog. I always hated those kinds of guys.

N: That's always been a big thing for me. I think it's because of my parents. I don't have an infidelity channel. Even when I was at my youngest and randiest—say, age eighteen to twenty-five. I remember having a girlfriend in college and thinking other young women were attractive. But it never occurred to me. It wasn't like I made a cognitive choice—"You should be true to your relationship." I just didn't have that channel.

M: You really don't. There have been so many times throughout the course of our relationship when we've been out in public somewhere and some really good-looking woman has walked by, and I'M looking at her, and I always clock Nick to see if he's looking, and he never fucking is. He doesn't even notice. Which is great. *(Laughs)* Because every other guy I dated definitely did. I love that you don't have that chip.

N: I just think that's only decent.

M: Oh boy. Dad, I want to kiss. I love you. You're a good man.

N: I'm embarrassed.

M: *(Laughs)* Let's do the next one. AGE DIFFERENCE!

N: Aha.

M: It's sort of a nonissue.

N: The story is there's no story. I was born in June of 1970.

M: I was born in November of 1989.

(Both laugh)

N: When we met—the whole time we've known each other—we've always felt normal. We felt like two people.

M: It's just like Mark and Nikki from *90 Day Fiancé*!

(Laughter)

M: I've never noticed a cultural gap. For example, I once dated a guy who was ten years younger than me. I said something about Aretha Franklin, and he said, "Who?" And I said, "BYEEEEE."

N: Here's your hat.

M: Yeah. Here's your hat, what's your hurry?
Once I got to be about thirty, younger men suddenly started to pursue me. I could never find someone my age or older. They were always younger. And I was

pretty sick of it. Not for any particular reason—I just thought, "Why do they have to be younger? What's the deal? Let's mix it up." So I met Nick, and I thought, "This is good, because I'm forty-one, and he's probably thirty-seven or thirty-eight, so at least that's in the ballpark." So we were driving along one day, and I don't know how it came up, but I said, "Wait, how old are you?" And he said, "Twenty-nine," and I said these two words: "You. Motherfucker." And I almost crashed my car into a tree. I was really mad about it.

(Both laugh)

M: He seemed older.

N: I have all the ignorance of a man ten years my senior.

M: I thought you looked older. *(Laughs)* Let me rephrase that—it wasn't that he looked older, it was that he was so dang manly. And I was used to dating these boyish gay guys. He also has a very mature disposition.

N: *(Laughs)* I have to giggle at that accusation.

M: Most of the time.

N: *(Fart noise)* It's funny; people in our circle—just a few—said things to me when we were getting into it. Things like, "Are you sure the age difference isn't going to be an issue?" And, "Are you OK with Megan being such a massive breadwinner—and you being a some-time actor/carpenter?" And I said, "Who cares? We're in love." *(Laughs)*

M: But back to your perceived age—for the many years we were first together, I think we even looked about the same age. Maybe we still do-ish. I don't know. But that helped with other people's potential judgments.

N: There's a lot on social media, too, especially when we work together as actors. People have often said of Ron and Tammy that they can't believe I'm not the older one from looking at us.

M: Issues around age are so ingrained in our culture, and it's not healthy. But can we talk about an aspect of this that is so lame? Younger people who think older people are gross. It's insane! What do they think is going to happen to them? Anyone who subscribes to that cult of youth is a fucking idiot, as far as I'm concerned. It's a hilarious lack of foresight in the most basic possible way imaginable.

N: It's like the health care issue. All the healthy people are like, "I ain't paying into that shit!"

M: Should we talk about children versus no children?

N: Sure. We don't have children.

M: Wait, we don't? What are those little furry things running around on the carpet?

N: Those are dogs.

M: Now you tell me.

N: I come from a big family. I have three siblings, and the extended family in the tri-county area—that's Grundy,

Kendall, and Will counties in Illinois—it's a family of public servants and salt-of-the-earth farmers, nurses, schoolteachers, librarians, paramedics. Everybody has two to four kids. That was my machinery, that was what I was set up to achieve. "I'll get married, and then I'll have some kids."
We tried for a couple of years. And it didn't work out biologically.

M: We didn't start trying until we got engaged, so I think I was forty-three. So it was a little late. And it was a bit of a two-sided affair, because Nick didn't have the trillions of sperm one might have hoped for.

N: Let's put that . . .

M: Let's just call that . . . Nick doesn't have enough sperm. Nick has a low sperm count.

N: Let's put that on the back cover.

(Both laugh)

N: Is it cool if we blurb our own book?
Like so many things about our unlikely matchup, on paper, the cold cognitive reasoning—sometimes if one partner wants kids and the other doesn't, then the relationship doesn't work out.

M: Are we breaking up?

N: Well, let's finish the book.

M: *(Laughs)* Let's get paid first.

N: We took a swing at it. Some of our friends were going through very intense in vitro at the time, and it was kind of fortunate that we had a firsthand account of their experience. It probably saved us a few trips to the experimental laboratory.

M: Well, with that issue I personally kind of feel like if it's meant to be, it will happen.

I felt like "if I'm meant to get pregnant, I will." And I didn't. I also never had a burning desire to have children, which is a crazy taboo thing to say. You're just supposed to want to have nineteen children no matter what. The whole mommy thing started to ratchet up about fifteen or twenty years ago, when every tabloid was like, "Jenny's baby bump!" or whatever. And I thought, "What the fuck is going on?" But that's simmered down a bit. Conversely—so I guess I was ahead of the curve *(Laughs)*—in a lot of countries around the world, people are not having enough sex and not having enough children. Denmark, Germany, a couple of other countries of note. But I personally just never had that innate longing. I think it came from a lot of things. Just a simple fear of the actual process of childbirth. What it does to your body, and the pain. I think it came from wanting to stop the bloodline. *(Laughs)* And the other thing is just a genetic disinterest in it. I didn't have that mother lust that many women have.

But when I met Nick—I'd been married before, and one time I thought I was pregnant, and I was PRAYING that I wasn't. And that's not right. If you're in deep enough to marry someone, you shouldn't be desperately frantic to get your period. It definitely might indicate that you're not married to the right person. But when I met Nick, I thought, "He'd be such a great father." So we tried for a couple of years in a really relaxed way, but it didn't happen. Things happen the way they're supposed to happen. And Nick has—how many?—maybe five other families scattered across the Midwest...

N: I think maybe six...

M: So that helps. But because of work, over the years, we've turned to each other and said, "What the fuck would we have done if we had had children?" Well, I probably wouldn't be saying "fuck" as much as I do. That's one thing.

N: We would have been those parents who say "fuck" a lot.

M: Yes.

N: I think you were leading into the fact that we were seeing other friends around us having to juggle kids with acting jobs, and knowing the hours we work, especially on a TV series, and the amount of traveling and constant relocating involved...

M: It wouldn't have been good.

N: We would not be present.

M: We would have foisted a child or two off on nannies, which isn't something we wanted to do. We've looked at each other over the last ten years or so and said, "There's no possible way that we could have had children and done as much as we've done in our careers." We've decided that our work is our public service. Or it isn't something we've decided, it just is. And that's sort of our baby.

N: We could have sold off our children, like Rashida, who every couple of years would pop out a bun, and it would be handily sold on the black market.

M: Rashida sells children? I didn't know that. She's really kept that on the down-low.

N: It's a great bloodline, so she makes a pretty penny.

M: I would imagine.

We did have a woman once—a woman we didn't know very well—offer to have a baby for us. To be a surrogate for Nick and me in exchange for a large amount of money, which she named. I had never asked her about it, or even indicated that we wanted to have children. It made things extremely awkward between the two of us thereafter. After we politely declined her offer.

N: Yeah.

And that, dear reader, is "Age Difference." Feel good?

M: Yeah.

DOMESTIC COMPETENCE

BY NICK

ONE PERHAPS UNDERAPPRECIATED KEY TO ANY HEALTHY and successful household is a properly apportioned, full set of practical skills. Sometimes domestic partners will have these talents in equal shares, and in other instances the lion's share will have been awarded to one of the spouses in extreme disproportion. So long as the combined attributes balance out to one whole well-oiled machine of a living space, and both participants are satisfied with their fair share/lack of competence and the accompanying responsibility, then a state of relative bliss can be maintained indefinitely, or so says me.

Let's examine my parents, for example, despite the discomfort this unsolicited attention might cause them as modest Midwesterners. I have known these people for nigh on fifty years at the time of this writing, and in that time I have seen them nimbly juggle four children, five grandchildren, three consecutive houses with sizable yards, a couple of dogs, innumerable cats, and two respective professional careers, all in

pretty impressively good cheer. For part of that time they ful-
filled more traditional roles, what with my dad bringing home
the bacon while Mom reared us cubs up to an age where we
could operate a zipper (sixteen years old, in my case), where-
upon she went to work as well.

With some ebb and flow through the years, my parents
have split up most of the chores pretty fairly. They are both
very competent bakers and cooks, providing us with agree-
able provender with an astonishingly regular consistency when
compared to (at least my own) more modern eating habits,
which involve a lot of eating out and ordering in. Mom is generally in charge of the oven, and Dad masters the charcoal
grill, but the cooking is frequently shared out between them,
even within the same meal. I am hard-pressed to think of too
many jobs around their home that aren't shared to some degree. Mom reigns over the décor, the laundry, the sewing,
mending, and the interior cleaning, but Dad is a good helper.
Dad sees to the garden and the yard, and tends to any task
requiring a tool greater than a screwdriver, but Mom is quick
to help rake the leaves. However, there are always interesting
deviations from tradition, probably in any couple, and my
folks are no exception. Mom, a small, gentle, downright elfin
lady, was generally in charge of corporal punishment when
we were kids, while Dad baked bread every Sunday and taught
us to shoot free throws. You just never know, when human
nature is involved. Their equanimity, to my way of thinking,
has to have played an imperative role in the success of their
child-rearing (four for four!) and accomplishments in each of
their places of employ—Dad's a retired schoolteacher and
Mom a retired labor-and-delivery nurse, both lauded for long
careers of exemplary service.

In our house, things are quite a bit different from the Offerman vibe I was accustomed to, due to our freakish lifestyles. Megan and I both have very fortunate careers as performers in film, television, theater, stand-up, books, and music, which require us to maintain a very malleable set of roots, as it were. We love our beautiful home in Los Angeles, but we can each receive a call at any given moment with a swell gig either in town or, conversely, in some far-flung location. In the last year, jobs have seen us scampering off to Great Britain, South Africa, Atlanta, Vancouver, Boston, Kentucky, and the Grand Ole Opry. We both enjoy touring as well, Megan with her (the best) band (in history) Nancy And Beth, and me in my capacity as a humorist, and sometimes we're even lucky enough to tour together. This is the main reason that we instituted our two-week rule early on in the relationship.

Even when we're living at home for long stretches of time, our filming/woodworking hours can be quite demanding, not to mention all of the other crap that comes with these jobs, like publicity and fittings and glue-ups and so forth. Of course, we are well compensated for a lot of our work, which allows us to be spoiled rotten, which brings me back to an examination of the domestic competence in our particular household.

I'll start with Megan, who is very much the curator of our living experience. Among Megan's superpowers, one would have to include her skills as an interior designer. She literally created our home from the skeleton of the house we bought and stripped down to the studs, with the help, of course, of some very skilled tradespeople who were not the guy typing this sentence. It is sincerely a masterful work of art. It is best viewed from the far corner of the swimming pool, all lit up at night, and if you don't believe me, you can ask our sweet friend Chris Pratt. Whoops, let me pick up that name I just dropped. Together we marveled at the vision she applied to every detail of the place, resulting in a terribly evocative whole, one night as we lounged in the twilit water sharing a cigar (not a euphemism).

This Shangri-la is somewhat available for your perusal in the January 2017 issue of *InStyle* magazine, and I should mention that Megan is greatly assisted in this effort by our pal Ames Ingham, a talented professional designer who is able to hook up Megan with "the good shit." So we have this beautiful and cozy living space with luscious art and fabrics (and the occasional woodwork!) that is further enriched by Megan's adherence to a very Zen "no clutter" policy. She laid this discipline on me when I first moved in with her some eighteen years ago, and I immediately recognized its calming value. Megan made our house amazing, and together we keep it neat and tidy, which subtly but consistently mollifies the chaotic energy of our schedules.

Furthermore, my wife, the curator, chooses the linens for the bed, as it turns out that you can purchase different types of sheets, sorted not just by mattress size but also by quality. What the F? There is a thing called "thread count" that I still can't quite wrap my head around despite a great love of arithmetic, and I thankfully don't have to because my bride has that shit on *lockdown*. All I know is that damn near every time I slide under the covers of our bed, it feels so good that I laugh, long and loud, at the pleasure.

Her artistic eye also extends to my wardrobe, which is another great service to our overall competence. I have always been quite capable, and still am, of choosing the necessary duds to wear to work at my woodshop or on a hike. Beyond those occasions, I simply pick out my clothes using the rules of thumb that Megan has imparted over the years (brown shoes with blue suit; don't tuck in that flannel shirt; shoes and belt always match; bowler and porkpie hats are never OK, despite how damn cool I think they look; et cetera) and then walk in to where she can see me and ask, "Is this OK?" and based upon her responses and my limited ability to learn, I'm proud to share that my batting average has improved considerably.

As I mentioned earlier, our intense schedules require us to be fed pretty regularly by other hands, and we enjoy the luxury of services that deliver quality meals that are healthy and custom so that we can maintain our focus on jigsaw puzzles and their subsequent photography sessions for Instagram. When we do have occasion to sully the kitchen, I am the one who dons the (very cute, denim) apron and fires up the stove or grill. I really enjoy it for the satisfaction of successfully following/deviating from a recipe to create something delicious and pleasing to me and my bride, and sometimes our friends for dinner parties, but I also really feel the touch of my parents when I'm in the kitchen, thanks in part to the fact that I'm often frantically texting with them while I cook. They are very patient with me.

I also represent the Offerman camp well when it comes to fixing things. I command the drawers of tape, wire, epoxy, and hardware, and I can't help but feel the tiny thrill of the challenge whenever Megan asks, "Can you fix this?" She is also quite competent with her fingers (nailed it), but my years in the shop have given me the edge when it comes to tinkering.

We have both been guilty of sewing on buttons or mending/patching ripped clothing, and I am thrilled that in the midst of this sometimes fancy-pants lifestyle we have retained the ability to whipstitch.

What I want to drive home is that in order for a marriage to succeed, the participants have to bend and be able to pick up the slack for each other, depending upon the proclivities of each spouse. Maybe one likes to rise early and one is more nocturnal, so the early riser is often tasked with business correspondence that wants to be delivered in a timely fashion, whilst the night owl will often surprise the farmer upon his rising with the large amount of work she achieved after midnight. It's all a dance, and if one dancer is clumsy and wears a thick mustache, then the other gorgeous partner must use her grace and flexibility to compensate and cover so that the steps may be completed satisfactorily, until the climactic final lift, when his worth is suddenly revealed and fully on display as he lifts her above his head, displaying for all the world to see the swan who loves him for his simple ability to carry luggage, withstand physical pain, and grill a chop of lamb.

Our house is very different from the one in which I matriculated, but I daresay that the domestic competence of Megan and me is not dissimilar from that of my parents. We are two pairs of lovebirds, doing our level best using what talents we have to add something to the world rather than destroy it. Megan and I make art of one kind or another, and my mom and dad have made so much produce that I cannot begin to list it here, and I'm not just talking about a shitload of cucumbers, although they are certainly guilty of that charge. With modest means, they have made a handsome home full of love, where good manners are the rule of the day but laughter is also encouraged. With their quiet dance in Minooka, Illinois, they made *me*, for crying out loud, and my three siblings, who have proven to be the estimable citizens Mom and Dad had in mind, and then some.

In the midst of our whirlwind activities (I'm typing this in a London hotel while Megan is engaged in a press junket for *Will & Grace*), it's easy to look upon my parents' well-tended yard and suspect that their comparatively quiet grass is a mite greener than my own, but I imagine that my family might say the same about our California lawn. Whatever the case, I am just grateful that they taught me to do the dishes and that I found a lady who likes that.

CHAPTER 5

That's Why We're In Love

Megan: Uh-oh. Next subject: religion.

Nick: I don't really have anything to say . . . *(Laughs)*

M: You'll be pretty quiet on this topic. I'll be doing all the talking.

N: That's like church and stuff? *(Laughs)*

M: Yeah, basically.

N: Oh boy. I grew up Catholic. My mom and dad are still probably two of the best members of St. Mary's Church in Minooka. They're a great example of how people can use religion in a healthy and positive way. They do it right. They don't ever talk about it.

M: I wouldn't even know they were Catholic.

N: They understand their Christian burden of service. They just apply themselves to helping others whenever possible. My siblings and I grew up going to church. I was an altar boy. I did the readings when I was a teenager. Probably around age twelve or thirteen, I remember sitting in the congregation, just noticing that when people would recite the Nicene Creed, there was no heart in it. Everyone was just like, *(Monotone)* "We believe in one God. This is what we say when we're at church so then we can go watch football." I was struck by the disparity between how people actually behaved in church and what effect religion was purported to have on our lives. I thought, "I don't think this is the faith for me." And that started me on a road that I'd call agnosticism. I feel like there really is a power, an omnipotence, that I would equate with, simply, nature more than anything else. And I'm certainly happy to attach a mysticism to it. I think it is beyond, and will always be beyond, human comprehension. But that's just Mother Nature.

M: I have it figured out.

N: Tell me! You've been holding out.

M: *(Laughs)*

N: You've watched me wander all these years?

M: It was a test.
I was raised—well, not raised—my mom was Catholic. My father was nothing.

N: I think he was Church of Dionysus.

M: *(Laughs)* Until my mother was eighty-eight—she's confined to a bed now—she went to church every Sunday. I know the priest from Christ the King visits her every once in a while. Father Stansberry. I was taken along to church every Sunday for a while there, and to Sunday school. I didn't get it at all. I had that same reaction—I thought it was so dry. I thought, "This is people's spiritual life? This dry, rote chore of a session?" It just felt like nobody wanted to be there. Even the priest seemed bored! So when I was nine, I got into the car with my mother after Sunday school one day, and I informed her that I would not be going back. To my mother's credit, she didn't make me. But she did have two nuns come over with a little thing that I still have in a drawer—people who are devout Catholics will say that's why I'm still alive—they gave me this little mildly embroidered oval with a picture of the Virgin Mary inside of it. And a little tiny piece of cloth that was supposed to be a piece of the Shroud of Turin.

N: What? You got a fucking pass?

M: I'm sure it really is a piece of the Shroud of Turin—I have no doubt that these two nuns in Oklahoma City just happened to have access to that most holy of relics, which they were allowed to cut little pieces off of in case a nine-year-old goes rogue. They came over and kind of blessed me on the down-low. I think my mom had them do some kind of hocus-pocus on me so that she could feel like I would be all right for the rest of my life. And then I was. So thanks, Mom! But I did get christened—is it "christened"?

N: Baptized?

M: No, christened. Because I don't have a middle name, and my christening name is Mary. It comes before Megan— Mary Megan. I was christened when I was twelve or thirteen, even though it was way after the fact of my bowing out of all of that organized religion.

N: Are you sure that wasn't confirmation? The sacrament of confirmation?

M: That side of you really bums me out.

N: What?

M: The fact that you know that . . .
But whatever it was, I did get a christening name. It's not on my birth certificate. And I don't use it.

N: I think mine was Michael.

M: Oh, really? That explains a lot.

N: Probably after my mom's dad.

M: So it would be Michael Nicholas David? Or would it be Nicholas David Michael?

N: I don't recall, to be honest.

M: That's a lot of power names going on there. A lot of white-guy names. You've got them all. All except Doug.

N: It may have been my grandpa Ray. Could have been Raymond. But I'm pretty sure it was Michael. But let's roll through the sacraments...check them off.

M: I don't know any—what? I don't know *one*. What are you talking about? I don't even know what "sacraments" means.

N: There are seven.

M: Oh god . . . it's going to be a while before you get laid, buddy.

N: You'll understand. Let's see which ones we've received. Baptism?

M: Well, may I tell my story?

N: Of course. I think that's what we're doing here.

M: This is when people will close the book and throw it across the room.
I remember being baptized when I was eighteen weeks old. And that is my earliest memory. I remember my parents carried me up the steps of the church. We hung a right and went into . . . What's it called? The nave?

N: Yes, the nave.

M: Where the baptismal font is. They laid me down in this cold marble thing. The priest came in, and he leaned way over and put his big, red, ruddy church-wine face right in my face, and he said, in a kind of baby talk, "I'm going to sprinkle some water on your forehead now, so I don't want you to cry!" And I thought, "You know what, motherfucker? I had no intention of crying until you said that, but guess what's going to happen now?"

I remember this so vividly. Like it just happened.

N: I don't doubt it.

M: So he put on the water, and I cried, but, like, loud. I remember my parents saying, "She doesn't usually cry like this . . . That's weird." They picked me up and took me out, and on the way down the stairs of the church, there was another couple coming up the stairs with their baby, and the woman was wearing a yellow dress.

N: And that woman . . . was Lady Bird Johnson.

M: *(Laughs, sighs)*

N: So you were baptized. Check for both of us. First Communion . . . yes, check.

M: I thought it was weird.

N: Fucking super weird. I think confession is a sacrament.

M: I kind of dug that. I thought it was cool.

N: Yeah, I did, too.

M: It's really dark, you're in a little thing, and . . .

N: Sometimes I'd try to go into the sordid details of my actual transgressions, and I never got the response I wanted. I was looking for some kind of shock.

M: Well, I never did anything wrong. So I had to really scrape the bottom of the barrel to find one thing that could be considered a sin.

N: I think I began to embellish my confessions so that Monsignor Seidl would find me interesting. A child of note.

M: He called today.

N: From heaven?
OK, that's three. Confirmation, which we think we both did.

M: I did.

N: It's the dogma, dude.

M: I did. I had a special dress. I was twelve or thirteen—I was a little old. As I said, I'd put a stop to all that, so it took a little while to get it accomplished.

N: When you're confirmed, that's when you are considered an adult in the church. It's considered the end of catechism. You can think for yourself.

M: Just another waste of a dress, in my opinion. The same as when I had to be a debutante to please my poor mom. Because her whole social life depended upon it.

N: It's only right. You're a good daughter.

M: Thanks.

N: Now here's where it's going to get fuzzy. I know I've got two of the remaining three. The next one is marriage. We're living in sin. We're not married in the Catholic Church.

M: No. Not in the Catholic Church.

N: Just in the eyes of Mother Nature.

M: But we're married.

N: We are married.
The sixth one is kind of a bust. I believe it's the holy rites. So only if you become a priest, I believe, can you get the sixth sacrament. Which means you have to be a dude, I believe. Isn't that still—

M: Wait, what is it?

N: It's called the holy rites. So if you become a priest, you become ordained.

M: You're not going to do that, are you?

N: Let's see.

M: The pope just said this week that he's considering letting married men become priests. Men who are already married. But if you're already a celibate priest, you can't get married. So the people who are already priests are like, um . . .

N: Fuck that, Fro! Step back, Francis.
So the Catholic Church is still THAT backward and arcane.

M: And women can't be priests.

N: It's an issue on the table if a married man can practice their Masses.

M: I don't get it.

N: That's why we're in love.
So the sixth sacrament is being withheld from the majority of Catholics. The seventh sacrament is your last rites, on your deathbed.

M: I don't think either one of us has had that.

N: I don't have high hopes for the last rites.

M: My mom's had that done, because there were six different times that we were told she was dying. So she's had them six times, at least. Maybe more.

N: She's good to go. *(Laughs)*

M: My mom really is kind of like a saint, though. Even though she can still look you up and down with the most searing look that just conveys—the most withering look that lets you know that what you're wearing, or your hairstyle, or your weight, or your face, or all of the above are not making the grade.

N: But I think she's a very benevolent person. Who's maybe a little snotty about appearances.

M: She's got the most incredible ability to stay positive of any person I've ever met. And her love for me legitimately knows no bounds.

N: So, for me—here's the thing about religion in general. Because of my mom and dad, primarily, I understand that you can live a full and rich life in the world and be a devoutly religious person. I feel like their foibles come more from just living in a conservative community, where there weren't any minorities, and there weren't any gay people out in the open. So they had touches—they had a benign homophobia and racism.

M: And yet they raised a gay son!

N: *(Laughs)* Don't call my brother that.
So I don't feel judgment—I don't like it when someone like Bill Maher says religions are stupid. I don't disagree with the Christopher Hitchens of the world, who point out all the bloodshed at the hands of religion. How brutal they can be, and how sort of tribal and backward and full of arcane thinking. But I understand that a lot of people need some sort of faith. Laurie Anderson talks about how it's all just storytelling. We need our stories so we don't go insane. And whether that's organized in a church, where everybody's getting their stories from the same book, or we make up our own stories—we all have our mythologies that allow us to comprehend the incomprehensibility of life.
The thing that I don't like about religion, and the reason I have such a bone to pick with it, is because of all the trouble it's causing in the world, particularly in our country. I generally focus on Christianity, on the bad Christians. Those are the ones who are simply hypocritical, like Christians in the government, who—

M: People who are pro-life, meaning they're anti-abortion, but they're for the death penalty.

N: Or they're completely hawkish . . . no abortions, but by all means kill the Syrians.
I remember when I got to college, I was just out of the Catholic Church, which I wasn't really feeling but I was still attending.

M: Wait.

N: I was doing the readings every Sunday. And so I had the dogma in me. And I also had been pretending to be born again for a few years, because the girl I was dating was born again.

M: You should note that I yawned at this moment.

N: Noted.
So I had to do this cognitive walk-back with my new friends, the members of the Defiant Theatre, that I met at the University of Illinois theater department. I had to say, "OK, you guys, here's the deal. I was brought up in this religion, and then I professed this further religion . . ." I actually had a transition girlfriend, who was also going to Bible study. Hilariously, her name was Tammy Schwartz. She was cool. She was a senior actress. And so we dated . . .

M: Did you ever tell anyone at *Parks & Rec* that you dated someone named Tammy?

N: I don't think so—it didn't last very long, so she doesn't really stand out as one of the main relationships in my life. But I had to walk myself down from this life that had Christian watermarks in it into full-blown hedonism with Joe Foust. He gave me *The Book of the Sub-Genius*, which is a wonderful, hilarious satire of not only Christianity but all religions, and also America, and, um ... humanity.

M: I didn't have any of those kinds of problems because it never dawned on me that I should feel conflicted in any way. But I was a weird kid. I believed in elves and faeries. All I wanted to do when I was a kid was play elves and faeries. It was a little hard to get my friends on board with that, because they were like "Um . . . nothing's happening. We're just sitting in a room." But that did not deter me in any way.

My belief system is closer to Taoism or Buddhism. Like a lot of people, I do feel that there are aspects of every religion that are important, and if you could somehow roll all the good parts into one, that would probably be a good thing. But in terms of the Bible, and being very literal about the Bible, that wasn't something I encountered until I was older. For example, Nick and I know someone who is gay, but he or she won't be gay, because he or she says there's a sentence in the Old Testament that says something about it. He or she continues to have sex with people of the same sex, but is convinced that they will someday marry someone of the opposite sex, even though they have never had sex with someone of the opposite sex, and aren't attracted to people of the opposite sex.

N: It's Beyoncé.

M: It is absolutely not Beyoncé.

In any event, the last time I spoke to this person, I said, "You've painted yourself into this crazy corner where you're going to be alone for the rest of your life." And the response was, "Maybe I'm fine with that. Maybe that's just the way it's going to be." And I thought, "Okay, sure. But if you could embrace your own actual human instincts and not be at the mercy of a sentence in a book, that might be good, too. Things might start to make a little more sense."

N: This is a good thing to focus on because we both became deeply involved in the theater at an early age, and theater has traditionally been one of the places where gay people can congregate and feel safe. For me it was a huge, eye-opening transition to meet gay friends and learn how their lives have been. Many of them had really traumatic childhoods, and some of them had come out to their families while I knew them. It really upset me on their behalf when the families wouldn't take it well—a lot of it is societal, and a lot of it is fueled by religion. That's a good example of something that's completely nonsensical, but it creates so much strife and trauma for so many people around the world. It's an example of archaic moments in these writings that are being taken literally. And discrimination against gay people in this country is one thing, but the insane shit that goes on around the world—genital mutilation, the torture that women have to undergo, the inhumanly sexist religious laws—that's what really riles me up about religion. That and things like the creationist sect. If you want to believe the notions that they believe, which I consider to be goofy . . .

M: And it's also so disrespectful to all the billions of people on the planet who aren't part of their religion.

N: Especially when they suggest that the tenets of their religion are supreme. Let's take anything based on the Bible. There's no denying that any of the stories in these religious texts have great value. They're great parables, great allegories, great cautionary tales to tell us not to steal, or covet each other's spouses, or kill each other. And that's great, I agree, we should all remind each other of these things. But to use those stories in any literal way, to presume that only your people are right and correct—forcing one religion's prayers into schools, teaching the Book of Genesis instead of science in school—those are infuriating moments.

M: I love them.

N: We'll work it out.

M: Here's the thing. You can't put the toothpaste back in the tube. Whoever the standard-bearers are for enlightenment, those people aren't going to become less enlightened. This is always reflected in the arts. Artists who create great works move that bar of enlightenment higher and higher. It can't be stopped.

N: It can't, and as two people who aspire to make good or great art—

M: Yeah, did you see me on *Breaking In* with Christian Slater? It was on Fox.

N: Did you see my NASCAR commercial? That was some great art.

M: That wasn't that bad. You can pick something worse than that.

N: One thing I really do regret is my three-episode arc on *24* where the whole story line was that someone had trumped up a lie that some Middle Eastern terrorists had set off a bomb in Los Angeles. And I played a pedestrian, a rube, who saw this news item and went out on the streets to enact racial violence against any "towelhead" that the character could find. It was a horrible story line.

M: I played a white supremacist in *You, Me and the Apocalypse.*

N: I daresay that the writing on that show was a couple of notches above the level of enlightenment of the thriller procedural *24*. We just lost a great many readers.

M: Kiefer just threw the book out the window.

N: It's interesting, in this crazy blue-red bifurcated national mentality of the moment, that the red side is much more tenaciously clinging to their Christianity, and the blue side, while not claiming nearly as much religious devotion, is behaving in a much more humanistic and empathetic way. Just today there was a big news item about how President Trump's proposed budget would cut the funding for Meals on Wheels. All of the reading I did about it from the left was saying, "Is nothing sacred? You assholes." One year of funding for Meals on Wheels, by the way, is worth about one trip to Mar-a-Lago. The reactions I saw on the right were things like, "If you feel so bad, why don't you just donate your money to Meals on Wheels? We don't want our government money going to this program." It's just inhuman, a lack of empathy, when it comes to things like health care or Meals on Wheels. Where this purported party of Jesus doesn't have the wherewithal to say, "Some of my people might get old and need meals."

M: They're all old already! Don't they need a meal?

N: Or they might get old and need affordable health care. It's quite baffling.

M: Anyway, it's all going to change. We're hitting critical mass, and we're going to reach a certain point of no return, where all this positive change we're seeing is really going to take root in the mass consciousness. I can't comprehend the amount of energy it would take to stay at the level of denial required to have the belief systems that a lot of people have. It's so gargantuan. I don't understand how people make it from one day to the next.

N: That's a great point, but I think because it's fear-based it's much easier to remain in denial than to have to be open-minded. It's human nature. Let's say you're prone to laziness and you think, "There's a beautiful forest outside my house, and I could go for a walk. But I'm just going to stay in." It takes a lot more effort to go out the door and do it. Once you walk in the woods, you're so glad you've done it. It's so much more beautiful and smells incredible. There's no way to compare it to sitting on the couch. You simply have to get out the door.

We both had an awareness as children of this opulent church, the nicest building in town, where all of our parents put money into a basket that was passed around each week, and all of these funds went toward paying for this opulence. We both noticed that there was no actual apparent devotion. There was no life in the celebration.

M: Well, there was no celebration.

N: And then we both came to find that celebration and that life in the actual live theater. So I've always said—I always get a laugh when I say it, but I mean it sincerely—that theater is also born of religion. And to me that is very religious. We both talk about how we feel like we have a calling. When people ask me what my favorite thing to do is—theater, film, TV, or whatever—I say theater because of the immediacy. You can feel the medicine you're giving your audience through laughter or tears or what have you. And the medicine they give back is the closest thing I've felt to some kind of holy transaction.

M: That's how I feel about music.

N: That's how I feel when I'm singing in the theater.

M: Oh my god. The end.

N: When I see the beatific faces, with tears streaming down . . . begging me to stop singing. But I think that's our religion. People of other faiths pray on a regular basis, or they follow rules of kosher eating, or what have you. We devote ourselves to creating the sermons of our performances. Delivering our own Good News, if you will, to the people.

M: Good sermon. I had the best interview the other day. I was doing an interview with a music writer at the *Village Voice*. She was interviewing me about Nancy And Beth, and she said that the thing that struck her after talking to Stephanie and me was that what spurred both of us on was this very childlike joy and pure excitement about what we're doing. And I said, "Oh my god! That's completely it." It's such an ephemeral thing. Nancy And Beth is like two little girls playing. There's a childlike excitement about what we're doing, where you don't realize that time is passing because you're doing something that you really love to do. That can happen with a lot of things. It can even happen when we're here working on this book. There's something mysterious and real about that. I hope everyone feels free to experiment with that part of themselves.

N: I think that's a great point. Because you two, in a way, do become possessed. You're channeling something. When a person can find what their calling is, what it is they love to do, there's something holy about that.

M: It's all of it: When we're picking songs, or when we're brainstorming what we want the record to look like or what we want the show to be like. What we want to wear. When we're trying out choreography in front of the mirror. It's full-on two little girls set loose.

N: It's a very Wendell Berry–ian notion, that you've found what makes you feel that way, and you thrive from it. I've sat in a great many of your audiences, and there are massive hordes of people that you've thrilled.

M: Well, that's very nice. And if religion is more amorphous for us than it would be if we were part of some organized religion . . . if there's some mysticism involved . . . there's something that happened in 2002. It was the White House Correspondents' Dinner. Even though we weren't huge W fans, we decided to go, because we wanted to see what it was all about. It was in a giant ballroom with about two thousand people. It was really just a lot of people glad-handing and networking, up and out of their chairs, all over the room, doing business. The only time they were quiet was when Bush got up to speak. They kind of had to be. But after he spoke, everyone immediately went back to working the room. And it was a bummer because there were journalists on the podium talking about colleagues who had been killed in the war. There was one journalist in particular who talked about a fellow correspondent and close friend who had recently been killed in the line of duty in some conflict overseas after 9/11. And no one was listening!

And then they said, "The evening's entertainment: Ray Charles!" And everybody suddenly got really excited. And everyone was actually quiet for most of the first song, which was one of his up-tempo hits that everybody knew. Then his second song was "A Song for You" by Leon Russell. It's a beautiful song, and his rendition of it was the most incredible piece of singing I have ever heard. The single most unbelievable piece of live singing by a vocalist that I've ever heard in my life. And nobody was listening. Nobody except me and Nick. And I started sobbing. I put my head down on my lap, and I was sobbing into my lap at the White House Correspondents' Dinner because it occurred to me that it doesn't matter if anybody's listening. Even if nobody's listening, you have to speak your truth. And here was Ray Charles, near the end of his life, singing into this deafening crowd noise, putting his entire being into singing this one song for nobody. Or so he must have thought. And that was so moving to me. That was like a religious awakening.

N: It's like a truth teller, with people screaming at them, continuing to stay on message. One of the Wendell Berry messages that I love is that he is into religion and the Bible, but he doesn't like churches. He doesn't like what people do with it. He finds his evidence of God much more out by the river and in his pastures than he does at church. And that made me think of the feeling of how I was organically driven through the use of tools—I used tools for so many years before I realized I could make furniture—I'm thinking of these trestle tables that I made at my shop. I made them because I could. And when I made this joinery and fit it together, and had this magnificent table of mahogany sitting in my shop that I had made out of a stack of boards, I felt a similar feeling of euphoria. Like "I have done what is right. I was called to do this, and people can eat off of it." Megan's talked about it ever since we met, finding creativity in every part of life that you can. That has done me a lot of good.

M: You can find the creativity in everything, and you can find the humor in everything.

N: I don't think that's very funny. But it's true, and it's less tangible in some things. It may seem a little obvious that Megan would feel that in her music or I would feel it in woodworking, but there are so many domestic places, so many little ways that you can make your existence holy in how you choose to treat your loved ones and your community.

M: The thing with Stephanie is that it's such a true duo, it's so completely mutual. Stephanie and I spur each other on. It's a great partnership that makes it so much more compelling and interesting than if I were just singing in a band on my own. This is more like, this girl and I have a weird proclivity for the same things, so we're going to perform them for you if you'd like to come see it. To me, there's some force at work there that transcends my understanding. Even though it's not a moneymaking proposition. It's just something I have to do. And Nick and I are also lucky to have the luxury to have things that could be considered side projects. Nick has woodworking and I have the band. We're lucky we can afford to do that. And of course Nick and I are a duo. Heart emoji, rainbow emoji, two-girls-in-cat-costumes emoji. Good old Mom and Dad. As we're going through life and we find that yet again we're on the same wavelength, I love that you always say, "Hey, we should stay together."

N: I feel like we should. Which brings us to . . . our wedding!

M: Whee! It was a simple affair. Just two thousand guests at Mar-a-Lago.

N: Yeah . . .

M: What a beautiful, beautiful night.

N: The Mormon Tabernacle Choir.

M: Twenty-one gun salute.

N: The setup is that this was the early 2000s. I am pleased to say that I don't know if celebrity weddings are still major fare for tabloids . . .

M: I don't know either because we don't read them.

N: But at the time, there was a huge market for Brad and Jen—lots of helicopter beach-wedding paparazzi photos. One of the first things we did together, romantically, was attend Debra Messing's wedding on the cliffs of Santa Barbara. And a helicopter buzzed it to take pictures.

M: Wait, did a helicopter really buzz it? Remember? Weren't they just really afraid a helicopter was going to buzz it so they moved the wedding to a more secluded location last minute? So I don't think a helicopter did buzz it after all. I sang at it. And it was pretty quiet.

N: That's right. It's the only wedding I've been to where they had the Jewish tradition of carrying the bride around on a chair...

M: We have to do that with Debra anyway. That's not just at the wedding.

N: It's like a monthly ritual?

M: It's an everyday thing. We carry her around.

N: And then you wrap a glass in cloth and she stomps on it?

M: We don't do that part.

N: Anyway, that created this traumatic potential that some paparazzi would somehow spoil our wedding.

M: Oh, you know what happened? We lived in this duplex in West Hollywood for the first five years. I'd lived there for over sixteen years, but Nick and I lived there for the last five—right?

N: Three. You must be thinking of Kevin.

M: I had another husband who lived there for five years. He was so great . . . *(Laughs)* . . . Old Kevin. Why did we ever part?
Anyway, we had just moved to our first house, up in the hills. We were going to a movie—god, remember that? Having time to go to a movie—those were the days.

N: Like a cinema film?

M: Just having time in the daylight hours. "Let's just go to a movie! Nothing doing. What do you want to do? I'm so bored."

N: Yeah.

M: No work to do.

N: No whip being cracked by any fancy New York book editors.

M: That's right.
The design of the house was such that you'd open the front door and see all the way through the front hallway, through to the living room. The far living room wall was all glass, and there was a view of the city. We're just at the front door, opening it to go the movie, and we said, "What is that sound?" We turned around, and there was a black helicopter, like from a '90s Tom

Cruise movie, hovering right over our backyard. Right at eye level. And we thought, "What is happening?" It just hovered there for a second and it moved on. A couple of weeks later in *US* magazine there was a bird's-eye-view photograph of the ridge we lived on, because a bunch of famous people lived on the same block, basically. They didn't even point out our house. We didn't make the cut.

N: Thankfully.

M: Anyway, so we thought, "Uh-oh—helicopters." So we started thinking . . . Oh, the best idea that Nick had, which was a foolproof way to have a wedding that for sure nobody would suspect or photo-bomb, was to do it during the actual Emmys. When I was nominated. We wouldn't go to the Emmys—we'd just get married instead. I don't know why we thought that everybody was so frothing at the mouth to get pictures of our stupid wedding, but we really thought that. So that was the completely foolproof plan.

N: Yeah.

M: But then we thought that wouldn't go over too big—

N: Professionally.

M: —if I just didn't show up at the Emmys.

N: But we landed not too far from it. We used the Emmys as our bait. We had just moved into the house. So we invited my family, and Megan's mom and Nat, her step dad, to come to the Emmys, which was exciting—it was your fourth time, or something.

M: Yeah, it was our fourth time.

N: We invited our families to come to the Emmys. And the night before the Emmys, we'd have a little get-together so everyone can check out the house. We had about twenty guests.

M: I sort of said it like, "We may have you guys over the night before to see the new house, but we may not, because that whole Emmy weekend is a big spazz, so we don't know ... We'll play it by ear."

N: We played them. Like a French horn. Even our assistant didn't know ...

M: We didn't tell one other person it was our wedding. Except for the man who performed the ceremony.

N: So everyone came to this dinner thing. We had a couple of friends each ...

M: We had to get a cake. I ordered one and I said, "It's for my mom's birthday, and she likes vanilla. So a white cake ..." The whole thing was just a big lie. We just lied a lot.

N: So everybody was over, and we said, "OK, now if you would like to step into the backyard, this is our wedding." People were crying. Shozo Sato, my college Kabuki theater professor and lifelong sensei, appeared from the back bedroom and married us with a tea ceremony. My dad was very funny—to this day, he makes a very sour face when he is reminded of drinking what he calls "that seaweed juice."

M: He has that oyster stew to explain to me.

N: He eats the most disgusting...

M: ...the grossest oyster stew. From a can. It's a mysterious family tradition, although most of the family has jumped ship at this point.

N: It was really amazing, our processional, as it were. Megan picked this song, Louis Armstrong's "What a Wonderful World," and it was beautiful. For the recessional, I picked "Picture in a Frame," by Tom Waits. And then we had a big party. We had a mariachi band, which was fun.

M: We had invited a couple of friends apiece. Sean Hayes was there. And we were all sitting at dinner—we had put a long table in our backyard—and at one point I looked around and I realized I didn't know where Sean was. The mariachi band had two dancers—a guy and a girl—in flashy costumes. All of a sudden Sean bursts out in this red satin dress. He came out and did a flamenco dance. Well, not flamenco.

N: He did a Latin style...

M: A dance-of-the-seven-veils style...

N: And apparently the ceremony worked. I guess it took.

M: It took. It stuck. It really was a great way to have a wedding, because everyone was so excited when we said, "It's our wedding." There was a lot of screaming and merriment. Most people were just in jeans and T-shirts. It was great. Really fun, and so easy. We had a caterer. I actually confiscated everybody's phones. This was early cell phone days—it wasn't smartphones yet, it was clamshell flip phones—but I took everybody's phones because I didn't want anyone taking pictures. Again, apparently we really thought our wedding was a high-dollar ticket.

N: And everything remained perfectly private until we got to the Emmys the next day. I will start you off by simply saying the name Shelley Morrison. *(Laughs)*

M: Aww, good old Shelley.
The day after the wedding, the day after our wedding night *(Evil laugh)*, we were on the red carpet. It was when *Queer Eye for the Straight Guy* was first on. Nick is very good at something called Spray, Delay, and Walk Away. Remember you used to do Spray, Delay, and Walk Away?

N: Yeah.

M: You haven't done that in a while.

N: You no longer like me wearing a scent.

M: I don't really, that's true. Just Axe body spray.

N: Maybe an illustration of Spray, Delay, and Walk Away would be appropriate for the book?

M: I think so. So we were there, and we saw a couple of the guys from that show. We were sort of friendly with them. We told a couple of people, friends, that we had gotten married the night before. And one of the guys from *Queer Eye* told Shelley Morrison, thinking that she must already know. We weren't really telling the press—just telling friends, "Keep it under your hat, but we got married last night." And Shelley raced over to the nearest person with a microphone, yanked it out of their hands, and said, "Big news! Megan Mullally and Nick just got married!" And told everyone. But that was all right.

N: Yeah. Welcome to showbiz.

M: We probably would have just wanted to break the news ourselves. But you know, could be worse. At least she's cute.

PICTURES OF US!

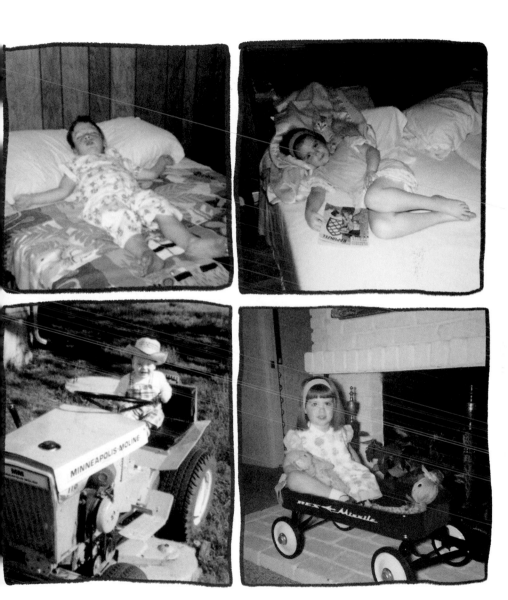

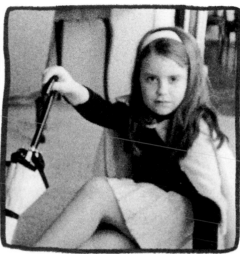

CHAPTER 6

Paper Doll

Megan: All right. We will now hold forth on the subjects of fashion, music, and art.

Let's start with art, shall we?

Nick: I have a bachelor of fine arts degree, so I guess I should do most of the talking on the art chapter. And you can just chime in.

M: Did you plan that line out when I told you that the chapter was art?

N: Me? Are you accusing me of packing a lunch? Is this about art in the widest definition?

M: I don't know. I guess—whatever it means to you. How our feelings about art were formed.

N: It's pretty city mouse and country mouse. Or *Beauty and the Beast*. Mine I've done some writing about.

(Barking in the background) Wait—our recordist is having some trouble. Hang on. Are the levels OK?

M: Our engineer! She has such a big smile on her face.

N: *(Laughs)* I feel like I grew up without a sense of art *(Laughs again)* despite playing music in band and jazz band, and performing as an actor in school. Those are the main artistic moments in my life. It wasn't until I got to college and met my Defiant Theatre friends—that was when I feel I was really awakened to a true comprehension of art. Up until that point, I didn't know what my taste was, in a sense. Or I hadn't discovered my taste. And I feel like you have always had a much clearer sense of good art. I've always relied on others. I know what I love, but I never would have discovered Egon Schiele, for example, if you hadn't shown him to me, and I realized, "Oh, that's the best one."

(Both laugh)

M: My mom had a flair for interior design. She enjoyed that, and she was good at it. It was interesting to me that she would move heavy pieces of furniture around by herself, like she was moved by the spirit to create, which is something that I now have taken to doing in my adult life . . . moving couches around at two in the morning.

Part of her decorating scheme would always include art. My mom liked bright colors and cheery themes, which is something I seem to have inherited, but in a more modern way.

(Barking)

M: Listen! No barking. We're writing a book. Are you?
I remembered, after telling the tragic love story of
Pedro and me, tearfully torn asunder in the parking lot
of the art gallery in Santa Fe, that my father had a penchant for fine art and picked a couple of the pieces in
our house.

But I think this chapter is not only about art you can
hang on your wall or a sculpture you can put in your
garden, but about art in the larger sense of creativity
and the forms it can take. However, I will say that
when I was about eight or nine, my parents subscribed
to *Time* magazine, and they had done a story on Yoko
Ono. I'm sure it was in black and white—that's how I
remember it anyway—and it really appealed to me.
She was the first woman who was a conceptual artist
of note, and her art appealed to my young brain because it was simple, and vivid in its simplicity.

That started me on a train of young thought about art.
And then I studied art history in college, even though I
only went to college for two years.

N: Oh, so . . .

M: I do not have a bachelor of the arts.

N: OK, I'll jump back in here. (*Clears throat*)

M: I'm a college dropout.

N: Picasso was an art—

M: An art person.

N: They call them artists.

M: Wow, I'm really out of my depth here.

M: On to music. Dad, sing something.

N: Sing something? *(Singing)* "I'd rather have a paper doll that I could call my own, a doll that other fellows cannot steal..."

M: *(Claps)* Beautiful. That was a nice choice. What made you think of that one?

N: I didn't really think about it. That's just what came out.

M: You'd rather have a paper doll? That's what you're try- ing to tell me?

N: *(Laughs)* No, it's just my ongoing Mills Brothers chan- nel. Just streaming, beneath the surface.

M: I love the Mills Brothers so much.

N: That's a sad song about a lonely guy.

M: Yeah. You must have it pretty tough over there, three inches away from me in the bed, with Clover nestled up next to you. It must be hard to stave off the lone- liness.

N: It's interesting—music is a huge part of our lives, both separately and together, and always has been, in our own individual ways. But very rarely do we play music around the house together, or in the car. It's a real treat to say, "Hey, let's listen to this music."

M: I feel like I'm listening to music constantly, but it's not because I'm necessarily at my leisure. A lot of time it's work-related, like when I'm archiving music for Nancy And Beth purposes. I'm also cleaning out my iTunes, which I started seventeen months ago—PS, I am still not done. But I will say that since we've had a record player, I've been listening to a lot more music for recreational purposes. I definitely don't like digital the way I like analog. I think that's been a lot of the problem with listening for pleasure in recent years.

N: Me, too. I agree. You've been a singer and a professional musician ever since you were a kid doing musicals. That was your big break—singing in the chapel in your school. That's how you got discovered by the priests.

M: Episcopalian—so whatever they're called ...

N: I used to religiously listen to music in the car.

M: Yeah, me, too! *Morning Becomes Eclectic* when Chris Douridas was doing it. Pre–cell phones.

N: Very specifically—once you could plug an iPod into your car, I'd listen to NPR in the morning, but then through my afternoon commuting, I'd listen to all my favorite bands.
But what I'm driving at—it used to be a huge thing. But my life had so much more of a singular focus. I just had to get to the shop, and I was making something at the

shop, and maybe I had an audition or something. And
that's it. That was as complicated as my life was.

And now I can't always afford the escapism, the brain
space. I need that time in the car now. It's become very
valuable time for phone calls. But also listening to
stuff I need to listen to, whether it's as simple as the
news or music for some project, especially since I've
started performing songs. I much more rarely now
throw on a Neil Young record or something.

M: I do still listen to music in my car, especially if I'm
with Stephanie. Recently, we blasted Nancy And Beth
with the windows down and were singing along in
harmony. Some people on the sidewalk started dancing, and we were all connected for a second. It was
nice. I love that emotional place that music can take
you to.

N: You've talked a lot about how influenced you are by
many different kinds of music. To me, it's part of us—
part of the fact that we met and had an attraction,
first as friends, and then as a little more, and hopefully
someday as lovers.

M: Let's not get ahead of ourselves.

N: *(Quietly)* Okay . . . My whole theater career was fueled
by the music of Tom Waits and, a second tier, the music
of Brecht/Weill, theatrical oom-pah-pah music. My
theater company in Chicago—we used as much Tom
Waits as we could. And I was obsessed with his body of
work, and that was one of the first things that passed

between us as currency. You had just recorded your first record with Supreme Music Program, your first band . . .

M: Well, one of the first things that happened—when we were backstage at the Evidence Room—is that I sang "In the Gloaming" into your ear. And that was a big turning point.
Then I played "Ruby's Arms" for you in the car. And that was pretty much the end for you.

N: That was it. Cupid had put away his arrow and pulled out a nuclear missile.

(Both laugh)

M: "Ruby's Arms" is a Tom Waits song I had recorded with my former band, Supreme Music Program. And I think that record was just coming out, or had just come out. He said, "I like Tom Waits," and I said, "Really?"

N: "Check this out, big boy."

M: And I played it for him. There happens to be a lot of music in our lives professionally. I had done a couple of musicals on Broadway before I met Nick, but since we've been together, in 2008, I did another one, *Young Frankenstein*. And Nick started playing guitar a few years ago—it's been a long time now since you started playing.

N: Yeah.

M: Kind of taught himself, took a few lessons here and there . . . pretty much self-taught. And now he's really good. Then he started doing what became *American Ham*, which began as Nick wandering out onto the stage at Largo with no prepared material whatsoever, which I could never do. I'd have to be carted away in a bag. But it eventually became *American Ham*, and it had a few songs in it. And now his newer show, *Full Bush*, has a ton of songs. I finally got to see *Full Bush* a couple of times recently, and the songs are great, and his voice has gotten so much stronger. Like anything else, you have to practice.

N: It's a muscle.

M: Yeah, it turns out it involves muscles that need to be in shape. You just need to do it. I told Nick, "Wait until I leave the house, or get in your car—someplace that's private. And just, you know, sing out, Louise."

N: You have been a great coach. I can hear that I'm gradually improving. And I love, at age forty-eight, that I can still keep getting better at something like that. I am tickled pink that audiences will let me perform songs and not get up and leave, by and large. And so the notion that I can continue to do a better job entertaining them with music juices me. It makes me thoroughly chuffed, as Colin Farrell would say.

M: In our *Summer of 69: No Apostrophe* show we sing some little plinky-plunky songs. It's more like comedy singing, though . . .

N: Or Nick singing.

M: C'mon, guy.

N: But if we're talking about music—you always downplay that anyone knows you sing, but that's been a major part of your fantastic career. You're known among lovers of Broadway as one of the greats.

M: Amongst Broadway people, yes. But when it comes to selling a ticket for a band I'm in, that's when everything comes to a screeching halt. Because, in large part, people know me as Karen from *Will & Grace*, and that's it.

N: What's this band called?

M: This band is called Nancy And Beth.

N: And which one are you?

M: Nice try.

N: They'll never tell which one is Nancy and which one is Beth. Only Megan and Stephanie and I know. And we'll never tell.

M: Nick doesn't know.

N: We even like to put it out there that I don't even know. Because it's so secret.

M: Because he doesn't know.

N: So let's just say that I don't know.

M: That's a good way to put it.

N: Do you have a website?

M: Why, it's NancyAndBeth.com.

N: Nice. And you can see the record art—and do you have a music video?

M: We have three music videos that I directed, soon to be four. My first time directing. We did a video for the song "Please Mr. Jailer," and then we did one for the Gucci Mane song "I Don't Love Her." For that one I shot the whole thing on my phone in the Snapchat app. There's another video for Joni Mitchell's "Blue" that's very different in feel. And last week we shot a new video series called "Getting in Shape with Nancy And Beth," where we teach you the choreography to five of our songs, then you can dance along with us and get a slammin' bod. I love it. I really enjoy directing.

N: It's very exciting. Those videos are so dope.
Before we finish with music, I just want to say that I'm very grateful—I love music, and I love the way it makes me feel. In so much of my life, and in so many instances, I thought, "I wish I could play music for people." I used to love playing the saxophone, and I was pretty good at it. I loved playing jazz and big band music. I don't expect I'll ever play anything but funny stuff. And I like even trying that, in a way that sounds as good as possible. But I feel like, for myself, I'm just grateful. Music has been such a big part of my life. It

was part of me recognizing how I immediately treasured you. When you first played me that Tom Waits song you did, it was "This is over. Game over." But also, it ended up with the whole Jeff Tweedy side of things. Wilco is one of my favorite bands ever, and somehow I ended up being creatively involved with Jeff, even though I'm not that good at music. For better or worse, he values me for what I bring to the table. I'm grateful for the lesson in that. No one will ever say to me, "Hey, we're having a big show, would you come play some of those crazy licks on your guitar that are so good?" and that's okay.

M: You're great!

N: Well, thank you. I'll lay off that. I'm improving. I'm glad I'm good enough to entertain an audience. But just in general, the music you brought into my life—I've learned so much from your knowledge of it. I never really knew a lot of George Jones, for example. And I knew and loved some Randy Newman, but just a tiny fraction of what you opened me up to. And as we travel about this world, performing in all kinds of different mediums, I'm just really grateful that music is one of them.

M: It is such a powerful thing. We recently got to meet Willie Nelson, which was HUGE for me, because I had loved him since junior high. And we got to meet Bonnie Raitt. She was a really, really big part of my high school years. I learned a lot about singing listening to her records. She was top three, one of the biggest influences on me as a singer.

N: That's exactly what I'm talking about. We got invited by the venerated program *Austin City Limits*. They have started doing a Hall of Fame induction every year, and they asked the two of us to host it. And that still makes no fucking sense to me. How did we get to do that? And at the event was Willie, and Bonnie Raitt, and Kris Kristofferson . . .

M: They were inducting Bonnie, and Kris Kristofferson, and B. B. King, posthumously.

N: It was overwhelming. Mavis Staples, Taj Mahal, Billy Gibbons from ZZ Top . . .

M: It was the craziest night we've ever— That tops pretty much everything we've ever . . . Gary Clark Jr. and Rodney Crowell.

We were in an altered state after that. And it was so great, because we were in our dressing room, and we were kind of just staring at each other like we had done mushrooms or something. And the door bursts open, and it's Stephanie, my Nancy And Beth partner, and her boyfriend, Alejandro, who is a great musician who goes by the name Shakey Graves, and they burst in, in the same state of complete, ecstatic disbelief and over-the-top . . . just in a state of bliss. Basically rapture.

It was great, perfect to have another couple to deconstruct it with, to prove that it really happened. *(Laughs)* It was unbelievable. And we never saw the actual TV special. They edited this three-hour live show down to an hour somehow, and we never even saw it. But I don't know how they could have captured everything that happened that night.

N: We already told the story of Ray Charles at the Correspondents' Dinner. With Supreme Music Program, I saw you guys play at Jazz at Lincoln Center. You also performed there with Elaine Stritch, who you sang with.

M: Yes, my idol. That was the same night, the night with Supreme Music Program. Elaine came out and we did this great duet that she had just done with Barbara Cook in London. Elaine was such a freaking genius . . .

N: And I saw you play at the Kennedy Center at a new jazz thing they had going . . .

M: Yeah.

N: I've sat and watched an audience completely in your thrall, and I was a part of the audience. I felt like I was in the presence of a goddess so many times over the years.

M: Who knows, maybe someday people will discover the records I did with Supreme Music Program or some of the Broadway soundtrack albums I've done.

N: Sophisticated. Bitchin'.

M: Nancy And Beth isn't necessarily a full-on singer's showcase type of thing, but I think it's better in many ways because it's entertaining, and it feels alive.

N: But that's the thing. You can sing in as many ways as you are a character actor. Because you can sing these dumb, funny songs with me, and then you step it up to these pro songs, and then there's a touch of novelty with Nancy And Beth. Then you can switch over to a completely silent, packed theater and sing a vocal to *The Swan* or sing "Annie Laurie" or some incredible classical piece, and just knock our socks off. You just kind of run the gamut.

M: There are all different kinds of singing. The higher-end stuff—I'm glad I got that recorded. There were a couple of concerts I did, like at the Disney Concert Hall, or doing Adelaide in *Guys and Dolls* with Nathan Lane at Carnegie Hall. But mostly through Supreme Music Program. Broadway's a different thing, but that's all recorded, too. So I'm glad I've been able to record stuff. But at the same time music is a very private thing for me. Sometimes I'll sing just to work through some emotions. That was a big thing for me my whole life, really. I still do that when I'm alone. I don't do it when Nick is in the next room. *(Laughs)* But if I'm upset about something, I'll sing sad songs, and that seems to work those emotions out. And the reverse is true with happier songs.

N: I didn't really know that. I do the same thing, only I do it with passing gas.

M: I was going to say the exact same thing . . . the symphonies I've been privy to . . .

N: When I'm feeling a little down, I release some ill humors.

M: He doesn't wait until I'm gone. That's the salient difference.

N: I'm not as private. I'm more of a family man.

M: He doesn't have anything to hide. He's not afraid to show his emotions.

N: One slight tangent. Casting about for anything else . . . So far I've only made ukuleles, but making something that I can then play music on, and looking forward to making more instruments—I'm very grateful for how these things dovetail together. If I ever lose my dashing good looks, I can find solace in making beautiful guitars.

M: I wish we had a little recording studio in our house . . . just a little mini one.

N: Let's see how this book sells.

M: Let's see how *Will & Grace* goes. Third season, in the bag! *(Both laugh)* We'll build a recording studio in the backyard. Just a small one. Just eight tracks. Sixteen tracks.

N: Twenty-four. Fuck it.

M: It'll be a hit factory.

N: You can make a hip-hop record that goes platinum.

M: And you will use the proceeds to fulfill your lifelong dream.

N: Yes, I'll start my clothing line. Kanye Midwest. Yee-Hawzy?

M: OK. This is the topic where Nick is really going to shine: fashion.

N: Fashion.

M: Nick is so into fash—

N: I got this. I'll take this, honey.

M: OK. Excuse me.

N: Fashion. Let's start in Madrid. Milan. Let's start in Milan.

M: Milano.

N: Milanese fashion. Or *couture*, as we call it.

M: He can't get enough.

N: I mean, what would my life be without Stella McCartney? And Miu Miu, and all of my Jimmy Choo skips.

M: If I had a nickel . . . Sidebar: Nick was dressed as Cher yesterday, and I was dressed as Sonny. I think he was pretty into it, quite frankly.

N: No.

M: I think so.

N: I wasn't. I was into— It was like wearing a monster costume, like it didn't feel comfortable, and I was doing my best to cut loose.

M: Methinks the lady.

N: We were doing this photo shoot, and they were playing music and wanted us to dance. And I've learned to let go of any inhibitions. I already looked so stupid. I looked crazy—I was wearing a tiny little latex skirt and basically two Band-Aids over my nipples. And a wig, crazy heels, and an Indian headdress. And if you want it to be funny, and to work, you need to not think about how dumb you look in front of the twelve strangers taking your picture.

M: It was really interesting. We did a few where we were kissing and stuff. I think we should do it full-time. I would just as soon go around as a white male. Right? Because they're running everything. And you'd be the girl for a while.

N: I don't know. Maybe we could just be bros. Because here's the thing: you as Sonny had a charisma that was undeniable.

M: I can so easily be made up to be a man that it is insane. Like, it barely takes anything and I look like a dude.

N: It's because you're thin, classic features, and therefore malleable. I am husky. And so you throw me in a bikini and there's nothing . . .

M: Your legs looked really good, though, I have to say.

N: That's a nice thing to say.

M: When we did our measurements—they made us do a whole sheet of measurements—we had to go out and buy a tape measure and do it on each other. And Nick's calves and ankles are almost exactly the same diameter as mine, which is very depressing for me and casts a slight aspersion on Nick.

N: In terms of the fashion of it all, I've just never cared. I don't care. I understand it and I don't disparage it, and I respect it enough that I depend on Megan's sensibility to pick stuff and to help me discern the right dress code for any given situation. But I grew up a country kid, and I still would rather be as I am right now, in my Carhartts, a flannel shirt from L.L.Bean, and a T-shirt from Bohnhoff Lumber.

M: I think Fashion in the larger sense, with a capital *F*, is ridiculous. But the thing I like about fashion, lowercase, is—and I wouldn't really call it fashion, more like style—if you can be creative, if you can dress in a way that makes you feel good, and that is creative for you in one way or another, then I think that's great. And I don't think that anybody should ever make fun of Björk's swan dress, because it was genius. Everybody should be wearing a swan dress everywhere they go, or something like it. At least she was doing her own thing instead of being this cookie cutter walking down the red carpet. Because one of the shitty things about fashion is how they've kidnapped the entertainment world so that every actress feels like she has to look like she's coming off the cover of Italian *Vogue* every time she steps out of her house. The pressure to look a certain way, especially on red carpets, is ridiculous. You should be able to wear whatever you want. And the money that I have personally spent . . . and nobody even gives a shit what I wear! But I feel beholden, or like my good name will be besmirched or something if I don't wear the right thing. I feel too intimidated to not toe the line and go along with it. But when I think of the gigantic amounts of money that I have had to personally spend to buy clothes in order to go out and publicize things that I've done, it's nuts. Because people aren't giving me clothes, designers aren't sending clothes to fifty-nine-year-olds. I probably spent on clothes, to promote *Why Him?*, the same amount of money that I was paid to act in the entire movie after taxes and after paying my agents, et cetera.

N: I despise it because it's one of the things that stresses you out the most.

M: *(Laughs)* Can you tell by the fifteen-page monologue I instantly launched into? I will actually turn things down because I can't deal with figuring out what to wear. I almost didn't go to South by Southwest where I had three movies just because I couldn't face packing. That sounds like a really ridiculous problem, because people are literally starving to death as I said that sentence, and it is, it is a ridiculous problem, but everything's relative. Let's just put it this way: it's something that I dislike.

Anyway, back to our lifeblood, fashion: I love going to vintage clothes stores and finding weird things, especially T-shirts. That's something that Stephanie and I have in common: we both like to play dress-up in that regard. But I've never been a "girly girl." I remember at one point I was on a series and another actress on the show lived for award shows and getting dolled up, whereas Nick and I would dread it. And for women, it takes so long to find the right thing to wear, and that you're not going to be raked over the coals for. Because when that happens, the coal-raking, it's unpleasant. When everybody makes fun of you and says mean things. It's not fun, it doesn't feel good. So you don't want that. You just want to kind of skirt by. You don't have to be in the top best-dressed anything, you just want to get in and get out without having a flamethrower shot up your ass.

N: That's another great example of sexism in our business. The women are put through this and the guys get a free pass.

M: So it takes so long to find the right thing to wear, and then you have to pay for it. Most people hire stylists, which is even more expensive. I just do it on my own now, because it's easier and you end up looking like yourself and not someone else's idea of you. And then getting ready takes like thirty-two hours. And then you go to the red carpet and they take your picture, and you go home and think, "The selfie I took half in the dark in the car on the way there is four hundred times better than any picture they took on the red carpet." I don't even know why that is. Can they not get good lights for the red carpet? You would think that would be a priority.

Anyway, there's a lot of pressure. If *I* feel it, then I don't even know what these other actresses are doing, the really famous ones. If I were some young actress like Emma Stone, I'd be in an insane asylum. It's something I don't really want to spend a lot of time thinking about. I don't want to think about my clothes a lot. I have so many other things I'd rather think about. I'd like to read a book and not think about shoes. There was a great tweet from Karen Kilgariff: "'Shoes!'—the dumb." That's one of my favorite tweets ever.

N: I like to have the same garments for fifteen to twenty-five years. I like my clothes to be comfortable and perform work. And I like work boots that you can send back to White's Boots in Spokane and have them re-soled. And I don't much care for having my picture taken.

M: Nick has found his style, which is sort of a no-nonsense, rugged presentation with a dash of pizzazz thrown in.

N: The occasional pop of color.

M: But back to figuring out what your style is: Just take your time and try different things until it feels right. My mother was very much in the Gloria Vanderbilt camp. She always looked great, but that wasn't my thing. My father was, like, Brooks Brothers all the way. My style, it turns out, is "'90s beatboxer." That's what I've settled on, and I'm very happy with it.

N: You have an awesome, eclectic style that I love.

M: I love you.

N: I love you. And I love work boots.

M: Thanks for being my fashion inspiration.

N: You got it.

Booty
Tips

BY MEGAN

My Tip?

Forget about it! Don't have any. Don't have any beauty tips.

And by that I mean: Don't spend a lot of time freaking out about what you look like. Just try to be the best version of what you are naturally.

Eyebrow Party

Okay, one thing I would say, though, is don't pluck your eyebrows. I used to have the most insane, crazy Brooke Shields eyebrows, and when I did *How to Succeed in Business* on Broadway, they got this idea that my eyebrows weren't 1960-looking enough. So they had this woman come and pluck them all out. I grew them back, but then Drew Barrymore had teeny little eyebrows, and I thought, "That's what I need," and then they stopped growing as much. So just don't do it. It's better to rock a dope unibrow than to have teeny little weird eyebrows.

Epidermusts™

Take good care of your skin. Spend a little money on good products for your skin and use them every night. Just wash your face, do all the little extra things, and use a lot of moisturizer. Use really goopy moisturizer and really goopy body lotion. My mom used Nivea, which is like putting bacon grease on your face. Now she's ninety-six and has like three wrinkles. She looks amazing. She looks eighty-six. *(Laughs)* But she looks great.

Threads

In terms of what men think—don't do that sexy thing. Women don't wear clothes anymore. It'll be freezing, literally 20 degrees outside, and girls are wearing, like, lace hot pants and a CBD patch. I mean, if you simply want to be nude, great. But if you're doing it because you think other girls are doing it and guys might like that, or you get into bars or get free drinks or whatever— maybe don't. Maybe don't even go to bars. And don't get free drinks. None of those things are super high on the cuteness spectrum. Read some books. *(Laughs)* It's a wonder that I ever had a boyfriend in my entire life, because all I really like to do is read. I don't even know how I ever met another human.

So. Not. On. Fleek.

Not trying to follow trends and fashion too much is good. First of all, it's exhausting. And it's expensive because it changes every ten seconds. And the thing that's the big thing right now, people will literally scoff at you six months later for wearing. So don't bother about that too much. Get a pair of plaid pants, but not, like, twenty pairs of plaid pants like I did. And then just get stuff that makes you feel good, even if it's not what everyone else is wearing. Buy something weird and wear it. No one's going to care, and you'll feel daring and like everyone can suck it.

It's All Good, Baby

Try not to be too hard on yourself about your body—that's always good. The shape of it, the height of it. Although I never was able to really do that until, like, three weeks ago because I started out as a dancer, so of course I was completely paranoid about every square centimeter of my body. And my father had been so judgmental of women's bodies. One time, my father and my mom and I were waiting for an elevator, and there was a really pretty woman in her twenties standing near us, also waiting for the elevator. She was wearing some top and a pair of tight pants. She was really teeny, really thin. But the top of her thighs went out a little bit from her hips—just a teeny bit. My father took one look at her and said, "Saddlebags." He called her Saddlebags because she had an extra inch of flesh on her thighs. What I'm trying to say is that he set an amazing example, so that was good. He also liked to make lascivious comments about a couple of my friends when we would sunbathe in bikinis in the backyard in, like, eighth grade, and that was also excellent.

In terms of body image, I would just let it fly, as long as you're healthy. I think that's the main thing.

It's Going Inside Your Body AF

Food that's not processed is for cuties. If you're a woman, taking calcium and magnesium from a young age is really good, also. It's one of those semi-well-kept secrets, like what happens to your hoohaw after menopause. I only drink water and, every once in a while, herbal tea. Maybe because of that, I've become kind of phobic about water. I'm like a water hoarder. I always have to have a giant bottle of water with me. Ask Nick. He thinks it's realll cool. ☺

You Better Werk

Exercise is great. When I look at my mom's generation—no one reading this book is going to be from my mom's generation, because my mom is ninety-six—even the generation after that, like let's say it starts at Jane Fonda, that's when people really started working out. Before that there was just this guy, Jack LaLanne, who was a "fitness nut." He used to work out, lift weights, do jumping jacks, and people said,

"Huh. What a freaky little dude." So Jack LaLanne was alone in that pursuit. But then Jane Fonda came along, and everyone suddenly realized that women could have muscles, and everything became aerobics. And then it was step class, then spin class, Pilates, yoga, et cetera. My mom and her friends never worked out, and once they got older and anything went wrong healthwise, they didn't have any reserves, any muscle mass, so it was like one strike and you're out. And so I think it's good to work out when you're younger. It makes you feel good, but it's also great when you're ninety-six. It comes in handy.

Special Special Times

Back to clothes: Have fun with what you're wearing. Wear what you like, what makes you feel creative and like a bad-ass. Here's a red flag: If it costs too much money or takes too much time—out! The end! It's over! Unless it's a special occasion, like getting married. But even then—here's a tip—maybe don't do that wedding thing. That's a tip. Don't do that big wedding thing where you spend all your money on a wedding and invite seven hundred people. A) You'll be in a mental institution by the wedding day. B) You won't have any money. A wedding is a marker. Celebrate, make it a beautiful occasion you will always remember. But there's a way to do that that doesn't cost every cent that you and/or your parents have ever earned and that doesn't create a lot of stress. There's still a way to have an incredible ceremony that's beautiful and memorable. My favorite weddings I've ever been to were, like, in someone's living room. That whole wedding thing . . . it's become an industry, sucking you in just like the red carpet, the way it's sucked celebrities in so that designers can promote their clothes. It's not cute. Find the cute way. Always take the cute road.

The Best Part

In terms of your sexuality when you're single, if it's a consensual situation, and you really like the person and don't think the person is going to turn out to be a major sociopath, then I would have sex with them, if that's what the vibe is. If that's the flow. Why not? It's great. Sex is great. If you're a sex addict, and you're crazy, then that's not what I'm talking about. I'm not talking about people who need to have sex eight times a day. Except for me and Nick. But if you meet somebody and you like each other, male or female, doesn't matter as long as it's consensual and it's something you really want to do. There's no reason to feel bad, or feel guilty, or think, "Am I having sex with too many people? Not enough people?" And if you don't want to do it, don't do it. If you only want to have sex with one person for life, or no people, or three people, then do that. That's good, too, if that's what you like. I personally feel like having at least a few experiences is fun, because when you're older, you can look back and go, "Oh, that was fun. I'm glad I did that. That was really interesting." Or, occasionally, "That guy was a douchebag, but no big woo because now it's hilarious." And then someday you can write a book about it and scare the bejeezus out of them.

My Stuff!

You don't need any of that shit. Get a phone and call it a day. That's all you need. You need a smartphone. You don't need anything else. You need a bed. That's a good piece of advice— spend your money on a really, really amazing mattress. That could be my most brilliant piece of advice. An amazing mattress, nice sheets, a nice duvet, and nice pillows. Set for life. There you go, done. Because then you can just lie in your great bed and have sex with all those cute people you like, and read when they're not around. And Marco Polo your friends and make movies from your smartphone.

I think that covers it. Nothing has been left out. xx

CHAPTER 7

It's Hard To Complain With A Mouthful Of Puss/ Couple Goals

Nick: The new topic is . . .

Megan: The new topic is . . . *(Whispers)* sex.
Nick and I haven't actually had sex yet. Not full penetration.

N: Short topic.

M: He's working his way up to it. And if all goes well, we hope to get there by . . . What did we project? 2021?

N: Sure. Or sooner.

M: *(Laughs)* So, we've had sex. With each other. Because we're a married couple. It's our legal right. *(Pause)* You're being awfully quiet. For someone who demands I have sex with him seven times a day, you're being suspiciously silent.

N: I'm wondering if . . .

M: You'd rather have sex right now than do this? This is why we can't ever get anything done.

N: Pause. Intermission.

M: OK, we're back. That was great. Thanks, honey.

N: I don't know that I want to do a chapter about sex.

M: He's so shy about it.

N: I feel like it's private.

M: Somebody asked us to. The people demand it. So let's just make it all up.
So, how many times a day, on average, would you say we have sex? Not the weekends—just the weekdays.

N: I mean, we're well into middle age. So usually . . . three times a day?

M: That's a fair estimate. Mainly, at this point, we never have sex at home. Only in public places. Because we kind of got tired of just having it in our house. We like to do it at the Grove. That's one of our favorites.

N: The Grove, for those of you who don't live in West Hollywood, is a rather resplendent shopping mall with a fake pond that has incredible water shows.

M: A beautiful pond.

N: It's one of those ponds that has choreographed fountain shows to Rick Astley songs.

M: *(Sings)* So we like to do it there.

N: Where else do we like to do it? The roller rink is fun.

M: That is fun.

N: And there's an element of daredevil to that particular coitus.

M: Mmm-hmm. Really anywhere in the Hollywood Walk of Fame area.

N: In the San Diego aquarium, there are three tanks you can access.

M: Not a lot of people know this.

N: Let's just say that maybe we're even more closely related to dolphins than we ever realized. There were about five years there where you were calling me Flipper.

M: Let's revive that nickname.

N: They're not the only ones with a blowhole!

M: Approximately three times a day on weekdays, I'd say... five on weekends?

N: That's fair. That's an average, though, because it's usually twice on Saturday, ten or twelve times on Sunday.

M: Not sure about that math, but it's hard to do sums with all that testosterone coursing through your body . . . We like to do it in movie theaters as well.

N: And churches are really fun, mostly for handwork. This is true—we were in the Sistine Chapel at the Vatican.

M: Is that true?

N: Yes. And the Vatican is part of Italy, which is in Europe.

M: What?

N: Which is on the planet Earth.

M: I'm not following.

N: I follow Neil deGrasse Tyson on Twitter.
We were in the Sistine Chapel, and it was amazing, but the experience was pretty uncomfortable, because it was crowded, and the guards were constantly yelling at everybody. You weren't supposed to take pictures, so they didn't want to see your phone. You had to keep moving, and you had to stay in a certain area. So it was like getting on a crowded airplane where the flight attendants keep telling you, loudly, over the speaker system, how to put your bag in the overhead compartment. So we just pressed up against each other and started rubbing each other's genitals with our hands, giggling.

M: *(Laughs)*

N: And then we made a mess. I will say this—Italian mop equipment is garbage. Centuries behind American janitorial tackle.

M: That was last year that we took that trip. Just for archival purposes. So when we're arrested, they'll have the dates.
I think we're more affectionate in public than a lot of people. Or anyone on earth.

N: There weren't too many people getting fingered in that particular chapel on that day.
On a serious note, something I would say in a book to people—because I wish that someone had said this to me when I was a teenager, when I was overcome with these instinctive feelings of lust, they really affect one's life, going through puberty and having this incredible drive to have sex—all the propaganda I'd seen was about how to impress ladies, how to get ladies in the sack. There's a lot of popular culture directed toward teenage boys, or at least there was in those days. Back when a rated-R movie meant that you would see some boobs. I'm glad that things have gotten more mature in that regard. But still, I would say to people who are not having sex a couple dozen times a week like we are, it's important to take the pressure off it. And treat your lover, or prospective lover, like a person, and talk about it. Sex got so much better when I let all of this teenage angst roll off of me and said, "Hey, what parts

of you do you like me to do this to?" Getting into a casual, comfortable, and mutual sexual relationship.

M: I hope you find that someday.

N: *(Whispers)* Thank you. When I think about my early relationships—my late teens into my twenties—they were so driven by animal instinct. There was a selection process that had a lot to do with sex drive. I'm glad I made it through that period to where my sex drive mellowed enough so I was able to listen to my heart and my brain.

M: I have not made it through that period yet. Did I tell the witch story?

N: The good thing is that we're doing well in our professional careers. To have an oversized custom oven built, in a patch of woods behind our house, was not inexpensive.

M: And Nick is fire in that witch's outfit.

N: That really has done me a lot of good.

M: Let's move on.

N: That's it?

M: What else do you want to say? We have to cut this chapter short because we're going to get it on. Have to stick to the schedule.

N: That's right. Okay, get in there . . . slow down . . . um . . . try two of those . . .

M: You're not the boss of me—

N: Goddammit.

M: And we have arrived at . . .

N: Fighting!

M: Punch!

N: Ow! Will you shut up for one second?

M: It's a new topic. Fighting! Although I don't know what we'll say, because we've never had a fight. *(Laughs)* In eighteen years. We've just been blissfully happy. Just cracking each other up. He acts like Ron, and I act like Karen . . . everything's perfect. End of chapter.

N: Sometimes when we don't fight, we don't have sex afterward.

M: We're too busy having sex to fight.

There's a perception of us as this perfect couple, so we've always been paranoid that if we get into a scrape at the grocery store, it's going to be running on a chyron on CNN. That's ridiculous, of course, but I'm exaggerating to make a point, the point being that people think that we have such an idyllic relationship that if we had a normal spat, like people do sometimes in public places . . .

N: It would be like the Death of Love.

We're accused of being "couple goals" enough that it puts a pressure on you in the public eye—"We're supposed to be amazing. Shit."

M: I will say—we're pretty lucky. Early on, our fights were more splashy than they are now. Now they're pretty boring. But we had some good ones early on.

N: I feel like we have a real complementary set of personalities and dispositions. The RPMs I run on, and yours . . .

M: I'm a lot more mellow than Nick is. *(Laughs)*

N: You're all chill. All the time. It's hard to get a rise out of you.

(Both laugh)

N: And I'm like a fucking moth in a lamp.

(Both continue to laugh)

M: That's going to be the name of my autobiography: *Moth in a Lamp.*

N: We had to figure out, pretty quickly, how to compromise our yin and our yang.

M: I call Nick Farmer Joe sometimes. Or Grandpa Joe. Because he's so fucking slow. In the beginning of our relationship, we'd be walking, and I'd be like eight miles ahead of him. Because he fucking WALKS so slow. And I'd say, "Use your legs! Let's go!"

N: *(Laughs)* "Farmer Joe"?

M: "Pick up the pace, Geegaw."

N: And to his credit, Geegaw picked up the pace . . .

M: He picked it up, and I slowed down. We've compromised. Because I was walking at full-on Midtown Manhattan pace, and he was walking at Corn Shucking pace.

N: As one does . . .

Of the many couples I've experienced in my life, I feel like we take a lot less umbrage with each other. I took as a cautionary tale some of the relationships in my family, the older generations, that complain about each other. It goes both ways. The husbands would bitch about their wives, and the wives would hilariously bitch about their husbands. Once I got into this marriage—

M: Which one?

N: This one right here. That occurred to me—this is when I go to my friends and I say, "Christ, guess what the wife did today?" and I immediately recognized that I didn't want to be like that.

M: It's hard to complain with a mouthful of puss.

N: *(Laughs)* True dat.

The example of my mom and dad has always helped me so much. In terms of swallowing my male pride.

M: It's helped me as well.

N: Go on . . . it's right there.

(Both laugh)

(Inaudible for a bit)

N: But here's a slightly different tack. We never really fight about the tangible things. The physical things. *(Joking voice)* "You've got to stop buying so many fancy hats!"

M: I really need to stop doing that, though.

N: You're welcome to do as you please in the hat department.

M: Thank you.

N: So generally, when we fight, it's about our state of being at the moment. And that always turns into a perceived slight. Or just anything—dealing with stress on some level. "I need to blow off some steam, so what the fuck are you doing with that suitcase?" It has nothing to do with the suitcase—it has everything to do with our state of mind.

M: Just us being stressed out in general. And then some fight will start over something really stupid. Like most people.

N: And as we've said—we certainly say it to each other a lot—just stupid schedules of traveling and high-pressure performance jobs of one sort or another—I think we fight pretty infrequently for the amount of stress we're under.

M: Oh my god, I agree.

N: Fuck off.

M: But I . . .

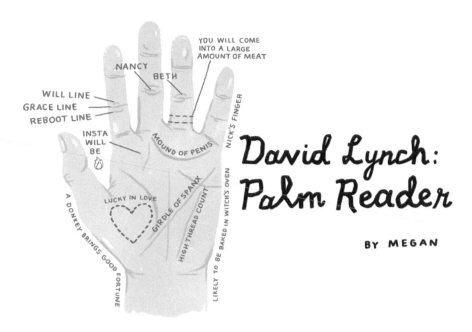

NANCY
BETH
YOU WILL COME
INTO A LARGE
AMOUNT OF MEAT
WILL LINE
GRACE LINE
REBOOT LINE
INSTA
WILL
BE
MOUND OF PENIS
NICK'S FINGER
A DONKEY BRINGS GOOD FORTUNE
LUCKY IN LOVE
GIRDLE OF SPANX
HIGH THREAD COUNT
LIKELY TO BE BAKED IN WITCH'S OVEN

David Lynch: Palm Reader

BY MEGAN

I MOVED TO LOS ANGELES IN 1985, WHEN I WAS TWENTY-SIX years old. I had just done a TV movie in Chicago, which starred this young actress named Amy Steel, who I got to be good friends with. So I'd been in LA for about a week, and I was at the Beverly Center, which was like the center of the universe at that point in time.

I was in the parking garage walking from my car to the escalators when a car slows down and this man's voice says, "Hey, Megan!" I turned around, and it was this guy who had produced the TV movie in Chicago.

He said, "What are you doing?"

I said, "I just moved out here five days ago." He asked me if I had an agent and I said no.

And he said, "Well, I know this woman at William Morris. I'm going to call her—she's young and looking for clients. I'll call her and maybe she'll see you."

I gave him my phone number, and a couple days later, she

called me and I went in for a meeting. Her name was Beth Cannon. There were two other young female agents she shared clients with. I was twenty-six, and they were all between the ages of twenty-six and twenty-eight. They were all my age, but they seemed like my mother—they seemed so much more mature and worldly than I was that I felt like a little kid. It was Beth Cannon, J. J. Harris, and Elaine Goldsmith. They ended up signing me. The agency didn't want to sign me, but Beth Cannon went to the mat for me and said, "I really believe in her," based on nothing—I had no reel or anything.

And so, within two weeks of being in Los Angeles, I got signed by William Morris, which at the time was the biggest agency in Los Angeles. I kind of couldn't believe it. They started sending me a million scripts to read, and sending me out on auditions. They also loved for me to come over and just hang out at the agency, which is so funny. That kind of thing doesn't happen anymore. I would just go over there and hang out in their offices. This was back in the day when agents would scream obscenities—scream at the top of their lungs at whoever they were trying to make deals with—and slam the phone down in its cradle, hanging up on each other. It was very exciting.

The other thing they loved to do was take me out to dinner. They were all so young—I don't know who their other clients were, but apparently nobody particularly interesting. I had to be the least important client at William Morris, but they were constantly asking me out to dinner, which was really nice because I had no money. They liked to go to the Ivy and put it on the William Morris expense account.

At the time, the Ivy on Robertson was like Studio 54 or

something. You'd always see a bunch of celebrities. So I had been to dinner with them one night at the Ivy and we were walking out, the three of them and me. They had valet-parked. They asked me if I had valet-parked, which is funny because that would have been an unimaginable extravagance for me at the time. So I said, "No, but I'll stand here and wait with you guys until you get your cars."

At the Ivy there's a terrace outside, with tables by the side-walk. Suddenly my agents started saying, "That's David Lynch. David Lynch is sitting at that table." And then all of a sudden J. J. Harris said, "They're looking over here. They're pointing at you. Turn around!"

I said, "Who's David Lynch?" And they said, "Shut up and wave!" And David Lynch's table starts beckoning me over. So I walked over to their table. It was a big table, about ten people. It was David Lynch and Isabella Rossellini and a bunch of other people. I wasn't quite sure who David Lynch was, al-though after the fact I did realize I knew his movies because I had seen *Elephant Man* and *Eraserhead*.

There was a woman at the table who said, "Hi, I'm [so and so], I'm a casting director, and I cast all of David's movies." She said, "We're casting a movie right now." They asked if I was an actress, and I told them I was. They all kind of laughed like that had been a rhetorical question.

Then David Lynch asked if I could come in and audition for the lead in the movie. I said, "I guess . . ." I didn't really understand exactly what was happening.

I gave the casting director my phone number and went back to my agents, who were in a huddle. I said, "They want me to audition for the lead in a movie he's directing."

The movie was *Blue Velvet*. I remember reading the script,

lying on the floor of the living room in my apartment, and thinking, "What the hell is this?" I was completely stumped.

Then, a couple days later I went to David Lynch's office to meet with him. We chatted. After a while I said, "Do you want me to read?" He said, "I don't read people. I just talk to people." I said, "Oh . . . OK." He said, "You're definitely not a Sandy. You have too much of an edge. But there might be another role you can play." He ended up casting Laura Dern as Sandy, who was seventeen or eighteen at the time. And he did end up casting me, but in a different role.

They shot *Blue Velvet* in Wilmington, North Carolina. The night I arrived on set was the night they shot Isabella Rossellini when she walks out of the house naked, down the driveway and across the front yard. So I got to see that, and to see for the first time a street in a real town with the trees lit up at night to shoot a night scene. I was enchanted by that. I got to sit in the trailer with David Lynch and Kyle MacLachlan. David Lynch read my palm.

The next day, I met Laura Dern. I run into her occasionally now and I always think of her as being seventeen. David Lynch was very nice and very "Gosh!" His real-life persona is very different from his movies.

My role took place at the beginning of the movie. Kyle MacLachlan is in college, and he has a girlfriend who's kind of bitchy and clearly not interested in him. She's just using him so that she can say she has a boyfriend. That was me. I had about three scenes.

So the character is in college and he has this horrible girlfriend, who is me. Then he gets a call that his father has died suddenly, and he has to go back home to run the hardware store. He goes home, is walking along, and finds an ear in a field.

They ended up cutting the first twenty minutes so that the movie starts with him finding the ear in the field. So I was cut out of the movie. But I didn't know I was cut out of the movie, and I went to see it, and was like . . . "Oh. Wait a minute." They didn't let me know I wasn't in it. I just went to see it and realized that I wasn't in it anymore.

Plucked from obscurity on the sidewalk in front of the Ivy, only to have my indelible performance cut from the movie. But then recently, they reissued the DVD with extras and I finally got to see my scenes. And it turns out I really laid one on Kyle MacLachlan—I full-on French-kiss Kyle MacLachlan in that movie. I have no memory of even shooting a scene where we kissed or touched in any way. I completely blocked that all out, which is funny, because I don't think I'd ever kissed anyone on film before, so you'd think I'd remember.

CHAPTER 8

I Would Have Had Such A Good Speech

Megan: I think it's time for a car chase?

Nick: Yes. It's that time in the book.

> **M:** So, what would be the comedy relationship book equivalent of that, preferably as it pertains to our fascinating careers?
>
> **N:** ... When we were late to the Emmys?
>
> **M:** My adrenaline is already through the roof.
>
> **N:** You're welcome.
>
> **M:** What happened, exactly...? The car was late?
>
> **N:** Yes, there was a mix-up with our address and they got to us very late. They made the cross-town drive to

the Shrine Auditorium, but then once you get within half a mile of the place, you have to drive through a choreographed set of streets, because everything is blocked off. There's a long line of limos, and you're driving slowly, past all the picket signs that say "God hates fags" and "Hollywood will burn in hell" and all that. And it's getting down to the wire because Megan's category is first. We're able to tell from the map they sent us that we're going to make a large letter *C*—we're going down two blocks, over two blocks, and up two blocks. And we said, "We have to get out and run. The show is starting." And Megan said, "I can't get out and run in these shoes." So she jumped on my back...

M: You said, "Get on my back!" and so I hopped on. This is one of the many times I have hopped on his back when we were in dire straits.

N: We were running down an empty street—because it's all blocked off—and this overzealous lady cop is giving me a bunch of shit, because she wanted me to get over to the other side of the street. It was so ridiculous because there was literally no one on the street. But I complied enough so we got past her, saying, "Her category is starting!" We got there and they yanked her in a side door, left me to my own devices—they wouldn't let me in because we didn't have our credentials. I had to run around to the lobby. They were shutting the doors, and I'm saying, "My wife's category is up now!" I ran into Melissa Gilbert, who played Half-Pint on

Little House on the Prairie, and she was the SAG president at the time. She grabbed an usher and said, "Let him in. His wife's category is just starting." And I got in and stood in the back.

M: And I didn't win! I would have had such a good speech.

N: Oh my god . . .

M: Dude, you got dragged to so many crazy things. But turns out it was foreshadowing.

N: It's nuts. I have had the benefit of many years of Megan's tutelage, because she's jumped all these hurdles before me, and I got to watch her deal with the challenges of playing a popular character, having people want to stop you in public, and having to deal with doing press and all that kind of stuff that's harder work, that's not as lovable as actual acting work. That's a nice part of our dynamic—that I can handle all those things a little more casually than if I just came in green, because I've learned from my wife how to do things with grace and elegance. Whether I adhere to that or not is always a question.

M: It's funny, because Nick was with me from the first really big thing, the first time I was nominated for an Emmy, which was also one of the years I won. He was with me for that, and for a lot of other things that all happened pre–*Parks & Rec.* And that includes a lot of what he just said—all the stuff that goes along with being in the public eye. And a lot of the time I was going through that process, he'd say things like, "Come on, you're overreacting, right?"

So, we used to live in the Hollywood Hills, and we lived in this neighborhood that was just overflowing with celebrities. I don't know what the story was. But Tobey Maguire lived next door, Keanu Reeves lived three houses down, Courteney Cox and David Arquette lived across the street, and Leonardo DiCaprio lived at the end of our ridge. So from our house we could see his house. It was a crazily obnoxious neighborhood, just a lot of drunk rich people driving too fast. And those Starline tour buses would be going by our house every hour on the hour. Sometimes we'd back out of the garage, and the tour bus would be parked right outside our driveway. And I would hide—I would put my arm up in front of my face. And Nick would say, "What are you doing? That just makes it worse. You're just attracting more attention to yourself." Cut to several years later, when Nick's privacy was being invaded, and he didn't think it was too funny either.

So it was kind of fun for me to watch him go through all of the same things. All of these different hurdles, or markers. And some of them are very gradual. You don't realize that it's happening until you're in the thick of it, and you don't understand why you're becoming kind of grumpy for periods of time. And I would say to Nick, "I told you it was kind of weird and embarrassing sometimes."

N: You can't really know what it feels like until it happens to you. It's a phenomenon.

M: One of the things early on, when Nick was a working actor but not well-known, is we would go to some big thing, like an award show or something, and there were certain people who would come up to me and they would also include Nick in the conversation. And then, there were certain people who would come up to me and only talk to me, and never even so much as glance at Nick. And then, when it had been a while since *Will & Grace* had been on and Nick was in the thick of *Parks & Rec*, the reverse would happen. People would come up and only talk to Nick, and totally ignore me. So yeah, it's funny how we've traded back and forth, and it just depends on what's going on. We could be out somewhere tomorrow, and there could be a bunch of people who love *Parks & Rec* and love Nick, and couldn't care less about me. But then if there's a *Will & Grace* thing happening, people might be just slightly less gaga over Nick in that moment. So it's interesting to watch it swing back and forth. . . .

N: Let's keep it clean. . . .

M: Ba-dum-bum. We'll be here all week.

N: Try the lasagna.

M: And the fact that *Will & Grace* came back, that's just trippy in and of itself. It feels like we just went away for the weekend, at the same time that it feels like a miracle has occurred. Those two things existing simultaneously.

THE GREATEST LOVE STORY EVER TOLD

N: I'd like to say in light of all this, but something else that Megan learned first and I sort of learned on her arm before learning it more firsthand, is that all of the pomp and circumstance of award shows, anything you have to put on a tuxedo and get in a limo for—the public has this idea it's like going to prom or something. That it's like it's a celebration for *us*. And you pretty quickly learn that it's not, that it's a show and it's promoting showbiz. It's promoting the shows, and the companies that are being represented. And it's a job. Going to those things is a long day of getting all dolled up, and for the ladies who look so beautiful, like Megan for example, every single one is like a wedding, in terms of hair and makeup and all the meticulous preparation—because one of the horrible parts of this part of the job is if you make some mistake with your appearance, you're excoriated on the red carpet.

M: I hate it, how high-stakes the fashion aspect of it has become. A long time ago, Janeane Garofalo wore cut-offs and a T-shirt to an award show, and that's always been my gold standard. I wish everyone could relax and be able to just wear whatever you want, and feel good and be comfortable. And, not to put too fine a point on it, but anybody who criticizes someone for what they're wearing or how they look is a piece of shit. Happy-face emoji.

N: Although it must be said that we've often said to each other, over our many years together, that we do feel lucky that because of the kind of work we pursue, and get to do, for some reason we don't attract the attention of the paparazzi. We're not in the file of performers that people want to get a shot of in our swimsuits, or looking like shit in the grocery store. And that feels very fortunate.

M: Yeah, thank god. The paparazzi doesn't give a flying fig about either of us, and that's great. Unless we just happen to be standing right behind Mark Wahlberg at the airport.

N: Or if we're in the Meatpacking District of New York—we were once walking our dogs, and doing some shopping, and there was a bunch of paparazzi activity. And that was the one time I almost lost it, with a guy who wouldn't stop videotaping Megan.

M: Well, to be fair, I was naked at the time. Oh, also, you wanted to take your pants off one time when we were in New York. We were going to an *SNL* after-party, and Nick wanted to moon the paparazzi—this was way before anyone knew who Nick was—and I said, "I really wouldn't do that if I were you."

(Both laugh)

M: And he didn't.

N: I appreciate you talking me off the ledge.

M: Because now those pictures would be fairly popular.

N: But when the picture of us shopping in the Meatpacking District finally did surface, it was exciting because it looked just like a picture of Gwyneth and Ben Affleck.

M: *(Laughs)* I'm sure it looked identical.

N: I had to do a double take.

M: Yeah, it happens a lot.

N: Benji? Oh no, that's me.

M: Gwynnie and Binny. In case you think our references are less than current, they're back together. You heard it here first.
Slightly different topic, but I think if you're in the arts, the reason has to be because you're driven to express yourself in that particular way. You can't do it because you want to be famous. It's not going to work out in the end. And it's going to bring you the wrong kind of attention, and things aren't going to go well.

N: In a way, it's always a learning process, and it's always a work in progress. So we're still trying to figure out our career balance. Maybe because we come from theater, we're more game. Just the fact that you did the play where we met, for free, with a bunch of strangers. And over the years, we'll, say, go to Largo or UCB and do a show, just because people asked us and it sounds like fun. Or we'll do some dumb comedy internet video for Funny or Die or College Humor.

M: Celebrities! They're just like us.

(Laugh)

N: But that is in fact something that we're constantly having to wrestle with and learn from. Many people who work a lot in film or TV don't do these extracurricular things, and that's because when you say yes to things like that, suddenly your whole calendar is completely full.

M: Yes, and we made a pact this year that we were going to try and slow down a little bit, because the last few years have been completely effed in terms of the amount of work and the amount of travel involved. And Nick actually did do that. But then I hilariously added fifteen times more things than ever before to my calendar, so that I haven't had any time off at all. But we have a two-week rule—we've never been apart for more than two weeks. At one point, I was shooting a TV show in London, and Nick was shooting season 2 of *Fargo* in Calgary, and he had to fly back and forth from London to Calgary every two weeks because I'm too lazy. *(Quietly)* Because I'm too lazy, because that's what it boils down to.

N: But you also . . .

M: Have consumption.

N: I have a donkey-like stamina. You need a couple of days for jet lag.

M: Yes. I can't function on the lag.

N: And I'm willing to roll in to London for eighteen hours *(Laughs)* to get my conjugal . . .

THE GREATEST LOVE STORY EVER TOLD

M: *(Laughs)*

N: Tallyho! I'm back to Calgary!

M: Being in the public eye, people say, "Wah, wah," if you complain, but it's a job! It's like anything else. It just carries with it this other connotation, because people consider it to be this exalted, glamorous thing.

N: That's the thing. A reasonable person could say, "I understand what is difficult about that. But fuck you, you're getting paid like a motherfucker, so shut up."

M: I don't know if it's the money that people begrudge. It might be that, but I think it's other things, too. But in any event, the great part about reaching a certain level of success is that it opens doors and you get to work on cool projects with talented people—if you're lucky. But the being-in-the-public-eye part of it is pretty dumb. It's for the birds. There's an old adage: The good thing about being a celebrity is that you can get a table in a restaurant. That is pretty much the best part about it. I mean, outside of the richer advantages we've mentioned, in terms of just the walking around in the world part—it's nice if a restaurant is full and you say, "It's for Nick Offerman," and they suddenly say, "Yes, of course, Mrs. Offerman, we can fit you in at 7:30." That part's good.

And it's nice to be in a position where you could potentially be an inspiration to someone. That's the dream, the ideal. So when you encounter people in the street who are fans, it's a great idea to stop and be really present with them, and give them a little of your time, if you have some to spare. Because you can be a positive influence to a certain degree. I remember when I was younger and my mother took me to see some Broadway shows, I got to meet a couple of the actors afterward. Not even leads, just the fourth banana in the background. And if someone took the time to exchange a few words, it just meant so much. I didn't want anything from them; I just admired them so much. Just to know that they were awesome as people made a big impression on me. I've never forgotten that, so I try to be really nice. I even stand there with the professional autograph hounds. I'll stand there with those guys for forty-five minutes, I don't care. I don't care if they're selling the autograph. Because it might be cold, or it might be raining, or they might be standing out in the sun. I just feel like it's a nice thing to do.

N: Weighing in on that last topic—I'm pretty hot and cold. The professionals really rub me the wrong way, because when I stop and think about it—they're just parasites. I don't respect that as a way to make money. There's something creepy about it. Sometimes they'll have somebody on the inside, like at an airline, and they'll hit you when you land, sometimes at baggage claim. . . .

M: Yeah, I'm not on board with that. If anybody is standing outside a hotel I'm staying at, or an airport, or where we live . . . I'm just talking about if you're going to be on *Jimmy Kimmel,* and they're waiting there. They're just waiting for whoever. They don't care.

N: But that's just it. That's what they've chosen to do with their lives?

M: I'm not making a case—I'm not saying it's an honorable profession that's being overlooked. *(Laughs)* America's forgotten heroes.

(Both laugh)

N: Those guys really don't get the attention they deserve.

M: *(Laughs)* I'm just saying that when I see those guys, I'm going to do it, if only because they've schlepped all the way over there. I will say, there is a high level of dandruff involved. It's not for the faint of heart.

N: I do it sometimes, but I don't think twice about not doing it. And then when you don't do it . . .

M: I'm in total agreement. If you don't do it, they say mean things. . . .

N: Then they're assholes. They'll say, "Come on! I'm your biggest fan!"

M: It can get abusive. When I was doing *Young Franken-stein* on Broadway in 2008, I went out and signed after the show for a year, eight shows a week. It was a big theater—1,800 seats. They had this ridiculously claustrophobic barricade at the stage door. You'd come out, and there would be people to your immediate right, the barricade takes a hard left, and then there would be hundreds of people all the way down, minimum two hundred people every night. Most of the cast of that show went out a secret back exit after the show every single night, but I guiltily felt like I had to sign autographs. It was a musical, and I had about five songs in the show, and it was exhausting, and I just wanted to go home and find Nick and the dogs, and get in bed and watch television.

And yet I would stand out there every night. And it would take minimum forty-five minutes, but often well over an hour, and I would try to sign every autograph, and take every picture, and talk to people's cousins on the phone, and do every single thing that everyone asked. And inevitably, almost every single night—because one of the perks of doing a Broadway show, if you're a lead, is that you get a car and driver to pick you up and take you home before and after the show—as I got to the car, there would be one person that I had not satisfied somehow. I hadn't signed their boob or whatever.

And they'd yell, "Fuck you, Megan! I came all the way from New Jersey!" And I'd think, "I just stood out here for an hour and half, and it's raining!" Or snowing, sometimes. It was kind of frustrating. There were a few nights when I got in the car and burst into tears. This driver, Dorsey Parker, who became our good friend, became like my therapist. After a while he had to walk down the line with me to try to run interference. I don't know. I want to do it, and I try to do it. Sometimes there are people who take advantage, or want it for the wrong reasons, but that's showbiz. (Laughs)

THE GREATEST LOVE STORY EVER TOLD

A lot of the time now of course it's about social media. People want a picture so they can post it to their social media instead of wanting to meet you because they admire you. And I think there is a big difference.

N: You've been doing this a lot longer than me, so you had a sort of code in place. . . .

M: Pre–social media.

N: And it happened to me with the advent of Twitter and Facebook and Snapchat, and all that shit. That's what rubs me the wrong way. Generally, when people approach me, three-quarters of them will open with, "Hey, can I get a picture?" And I say, "No!" If I'm not rushing to my airplane or something, I'll say, "No, thank you, but what's your name?" I try to be friendly and say, "If you're my fan, I want to meet you, and say thank you for supporting me." And I say to them, don't open with, "Can I get a picture?" Because that makes me feel like a zoo animal or a cardboard cutout. If you're interested in me, let's meet. Then I'll take a damn picture. But understand that we're human beings, and respect that if I'm walking through the airport—which is where I get it the worst—it tries my patience, because I'm usually dealing with something like, "I have to call my brother." Or, "Something's going on at work." I have to get to my gate so I can deal with a situation, and somebody stops you, and there's a real sense of entitlement, where especially young people will express their displeasure when you deny them scoring their social media points.

M: Nick says, frequently, "I'll have a conversation with you, but I'd rather not take a picture." Sometimes that's how he feels, and I think it's cool that he's able to be honest about it.

N: At book signings, I had to make a rule, almost immediately, when I wrote my first book, "No more phones." Everyone was coming up and making it all about what they were going to put on their social media. And I thought, "I came here to Kansas City to shake your hand and sign your book. And all you care about is getting some funny picture. So if I see your phones, you have to leave. That's my rule."

M: It's a tough one. I try to give as much of my time as I can, because I would appreciate that if the tables were turned, but it definitely depends on the time and the place, and the person, and how it's handled. And the amount of alcohol involved. *(Laughs)* Sometimes the drunkies are a bit much. And also, it sounds like fake news, but literally NO ONE'S CAMERA EVER WORKS. I think people get nervous, and then it's minimum three tries to get an actual photo in the can. I mean, personally, I would be embarrassed to ask someone for a selfie, I think it's lame. Although I did just take one with Jeff Probst. *(Both laugh)*

N: But the thing is, you have respect. So you wouldn't go up to someone you admire and say, "Hey, could you do a video for my cousin?" I'm with you, and I have learned a lot of that from you, but at the same time, I think people are really rude, especially with their social media.

So I don't want to say, "Oh, yeah, absolutely! Finger me! Touch my beard!" *(Laughs)*

M: I let people finger me, but I don't let them touch my beard.

N: Well, that's why we have such complementary personalities.

M: I have a good story about award shows and how they can be a lot of work, *and* it involves a glorious movie star. Everybody wins! I was at the Golden Globes. I was nominated, and that year I was also presenting. The Golden Globes is hilarious, because it's at the Beverly Hilton in Los Angeles, and the room is half the size it needs to be to accommodate the number of people.

N: You're referring to Merv Griffin's Beverly Hilton?

M: Merv's place, we call it.
Everybody's packed in like sardines. And there's a caste system, and the movie people are at the top of the heap.

N: The room is actually terraced.

M: The movie people are front and center, and the TV people are relegated to the galleys, and everybody's mashed together. There was one year I almost felt like my ribs might get broken—my stomach was mashed up against the table, and the back of my chair was mashed up against the back of someone else's chair, and that person's rib cage was also mashed up against their table. It's close quarters, I guess is what I'm saying.

That year I was seated very close to the stage left exit to the backstage area. And when it got to be the segment before I was supposed to present, they came to get me. I'm not a drinker, but that night I had a glass of wine. It was in my hand when they said, "We have to take you backstage." So I said, "OK," and gave Nick a kiss and said, "See you later."

As I entered the backstage area, I came around the corner, with my wine, and Meryl Streep was standing right there, just by herself. I had never spoken to her. I had only seen her in the front row one year at the SAG Awards when I won and I was walking up to accept the award, and I was so excited to see Meryl Streep that I fell on my face on live television. It was worth it. Believe me.

So I turned the corner, and there is Meryl Streep. I said, "Hi," and she said, "Hello." I said, "I don't know why I brought my glass of wine, but here it is." She just looked at me, raised one eyebrow, and said, "How else are you going to get through it?"

I thought, "I knew you were going to be amazing, and you are." But that story really sums it up.

N: There it is.

M: Let's just recap. Things don't go from point A to point B in an unbroken straight line. You might have dreams or aspirations, but it might not happen in the timing you're expecting, and it also might take a circuitous route. But

I really believe that if you really want something, and you hone your talents and skills and persevere and seize opportunities when they come your way, eventually it will happen in some way, shape, or form. It's just really interesting—all the different things we've been able to do, and the cool people we've gotten to meet and work with. And it's fascinating how few crazy people we have encountered—because I know they're out there. There have been a couple of doozies, but for the most part, everyone is surprisingly cool.

N: Knock on wood. We've had a very friendly ride so far.

M: Somebody told me a long time ago that a lot of people who have had longevity in their careers are also relatively nice, normal people, because producers don't want to hire crazy people. And if it's between two people, and one of them is not a bummer, they're going to hire that person. And I do think that actually holds some water.

N: Sure, I think it's probably true in all walks of life.

M: Peace.

N: Peace out.

M: This has been fun. *(Laughs)* But I think something else that you and I have in common is that we don't want to feel limited. We want to do more than one thing.

N: Yep, I agree. Even though I didn't start out with the talents that you did.

M: C'mon, buddy.

N: I loved playing the saxophone, but I never had a teacher who was an inspired musician.

M: Cut to: Your music teacher hangs himself.

N: So I never had anyone teach me beyond the rudiments. But your artistic—I'm going to take a swing at a word here—polymathy. Is that a word, "polymathy"? Like "polymath"?

M: I'll allow it.

N: I think that I, too, understood that the theater was a place where you can do a whole bunch of different arts.

M: I agree.

N: You can dance there, you can sing there, you can build scenery there, you can choreograph fights there, but for both of us, apparently, our main thing was, "Let me perform good writing." That became clear to me. That's what I wanted to do. When I did Arthur Miller's *The Crucible,* I was twenty-five, and that was a very seminal moment. I thought, "If I can just speak writing like this to an audience, that will be a pretty satisfying life."

M: That's something we decided a few years ago. I had a bad experience—the only really bad experience I've had in the arts, actually—with somebody who if I say anything specific will have me disappeared. But I had a very bad experience with someone in a creative endeavor, and I resolved the situation in my own way. And ever since then, Nick and I have said, "We want to work on good projects with nice people who are good at their jobs." That's the bottom line. You want the project itself to have integrity in whatever way—either the funniest thing in the world, or the saddest, or somewhere in between. And you want the people you work with to be nice people, good people, with integrity. But you also want them to be really, really great at what they do, in all departments. So if you're doing a movie, you want the best boy to be the BEST best boy ever in the whole wide world. So that's what we aim for, but of course that doesn't always happen.

I've always been such a late bloomer. I didn't even get *Will & Grace* the first time around until I was almost forty, and there's so much more I want to do. In some ways, I wish that I had gotten to start a little bit younger with things hitting success-wise, so that I had a bigger body of work, as they say. But it is what it is. I'm childlike in my optimism and the feeling that there are so many great things that lie ahead, probably to the point of naïveté. But that's how I feel.

N: I shouldn't be at all surprised. You can't stop one of the greats.

M: *(Laughs)* You know, we're talking about all of this, but then you have to put it into context. It's not Dame Judi and Olivier talking, it's just us chickens. But there is something mysterious about the creative process. At least to me, anyway.

N: Not to me.

M: *(Laughs)*

N: I think we've touched on this in other sections, but I can't help looking at our careers without being so aware, in Megan's history and my own, and also in our present lives, that we're the perfect laboratory experiment for how sexist Hollywood is. Because I think I'm perfectly entertaining enough to do a passable job in acting roles, but Megan is such a ridiculous package of talent in a way that I'm not. She has gifts. And that's why, from an early age, she was cast. She'd be up for a show, and they'd say, "Freshmen don't get cast, but you get a lead role and a song." And I didn't. It's because Megan is a star.

M: No. Oh, wait a minute, maybe I *am* the shit.

(Both laugh)

N: So to live in a house with a star and a donkey, and the donkey . . . There seem to be a lot more roles for authoritarian white guys—principals, coaches, soldiers, ex-athletes, cops—than there are for women over thirty-five.

M: Well, I do think there's more that I have to offer, sides that I haven't really had opportunities to show so far. But I still think I'll get to show them, which I said earlier. I don't know if I'm particularly an optimist. Maybe I am, or maybe some other word would describe it better. A dummy? But I feel like eventually I'll get to show more. But it's all sort of academic, because I've gotten to do a lot of great things. I've been lucky. It's funny when people say, "You've never even had a real job," and I say, "What are you talking about? What we do is hard, bro!" But in another way, we're just crazy lucky, because it is also 100 percent like playing. But if you're doing what you love to do, it's going to feel like play no matter what career you're in.

N: Yup.

PUZZLES WE DID!

CHAPTER 9

Fresh To A Fault

Nick: The topic is . . .

Megan: Keeping it fresh.

N: Keeping it fresh.

M: Are we talking about vaginas? Or . . .

N: Yes, please. Let's cross vinegar off the list, for starters.

M: Let's keep this douche runner for sure. It's too bad we didn't start that earlier.

N: It's going to be a big hit. In 1976.

M: We're supposed to talk about puzzles. And dogs. And other fascinating ways we keep it fresh.
It's pretty easy to keep it fresh when we have 17,000 different jobs a year.

N: When I think of the situation where a married couple needs to keep it fresh, it's where you have lives . . .

M: You're in a rut.

N: You have lives where there's repeatability, where there's a pattern. You're working at the bank, or taking the kids to soccer, if that's what it is. But we have really strange lives in comparison to nine-to-five households, as in it's all we can do to GET to our house.

M: We're not in our house right now. I don't know if we've been in our house for any part of this book. I think we've been in different hotels for every single chapter.

N: We're in a Georgian-themed bedroom in a fancy hotel in Newport, Rhode Island *(Both laugh)*, because we just played the Newport Folk Festival.

M: I played a couple of shows with Nancy And Beth, and Nick did a bunch of stuff, including two big dance numbers in our Nancy And Beth show!

N: But that's typical. Tomorrow Megan flies to LA, but I have to drive to Brooklyn to work on a movie. She has to go start the new *Will & Grace*. So our lives are kept fresh to a fault. And so we just kind of hang on to each other for dear life and make sure that we place our relationship as the top priority before our jobs. As previously mentioned, we have our two-week rule, but we rarely have to invoke it. Maybe a few times a year, we'll spend a week apart. But because of *Will & Grace* and this movie, we're about to have a twelve-day thing.

Then we'll see each other two weekends in a row, then we have a two-week-apart time.

M: Then we're together a chunk. But after that we've decided to take a lot of time off. Once every year and a half, we take about two months off. We're doing that this year around the holidays. We're taking a break to have real time together.

N: Again, I feel like we do a pretty good job—we took a pretty amazing month-long trip through Europe.

M: That was when we were fingering each other at the Vatican.

N: Yeah. So we've come full circle.

(Both laugh)

M: What *do* we do when we have time off? I think we've already covered a lot of this. On Nick's side we have woodworking, guitar playing, singing, fashion. . . .

N: Yeah, those all have to do with how I have survived, or sometimes thrived, while trying to get acting work, by turning other things that I love to do into a remunerative pastime. Or just a place of solace and productive consumption of time versus sitting in the bar. For me, because I was a theater guy in Chicago, I was brought up to go to the bar. I love the pub. I like to drink pints of beer and listen to music and tell stories. I love bar life. I had to really wean myself off of it in my thirties because it was just not healthy.

M: We're recording this in a bar, by the way.

N: In our household, I feel like our hobby, our life pre-server, has become doing jigsaw puzzles while simul-taneously listening to audiobooks. And it's particularly because of all the fucking noise that exists today. We're both lucky enough to be busy with all kinds of jobs, but those jobs bring with them so much noise. Like, we did a photoshoot recently and it was rife with emails and scheduling. We had originally actually passed on it, in fact, because we were taking time away to work on this book. And they came back and said, "If we change the shoot to San Francisco, will you come in from your writing retreat for a day?" And we agreed, because we thought it would be a fun thing to take part in. But there's just so much noise.

M: It's the story of two introverts who can't say no.

N: So doing puzzles and listening to audiobooks are two things that require us to turn off. You can't do either of those things and have your phone turned on, or any other media. You have to completely put yourself in a vacuum. That's what's so great about hobbies and dis-ciplines: for us it's a matter of health. It's not like we're sitting around asking each other, "What do you want to do this weekend? Let's do a puzzle and listen to a book." We say, "Next week we have four days. We're going to do two puzzles and listen to two books."

M: *(Laughs)* Well, maybe not that much. It usually takes a few days per puzzle, depending on the number of pieces.

N: Yeah, don't hold me to those numbers.

M: Now we're just writing a puzzle book. Let's stop pretending otherwise. We're writing a book about jigsaw puzzles.
Anyway, we do that when we can. This last Thanksgiv-
ing Nick and I went up to Big Sur. We actually checked
our cell phones at the reception desk of the hotel the
night we arrived. We said, "Take these and don't give
them back to us no matter what happens." Like that
scene from *Young Frankenstein*: "Do *not* open this door,
no matter how much I beg or plead." And we didn't have
our cell phones for eleven days. We didn't go online, we
didn't check anything. We did a lot of puzzles and we listened to a lot of books. We read books in hard copy. We
sat outside and looked at the ocean. The stars.
And it was also right after the election, so we watched a
lot of CNN and MSNBC and railed at the gods. It was
great. I would throw my phone out the window right this
second if I thought that I could get away with it. I've now
pretty much completely given up my computer. I rarely
use my laptop unless I absolutely have to. If I have to go
through and choose photos from a photo shoot, if it's
something where I have to have a big screen, I'll use it,
but otherwise I never use my computer. I do everything
on my phone. But of course I resent my phone at the
same time that it's this great convenience.

N: It's a conundrum.

M: I look back with longing to the years that I lived on
Harper Avenue in that duplex, the last three of which

were with Nick. I lived there for sixteen years, and I think about how simple everything was, because it was pre-everything-digital.

N: You didn't know what people were doing in New York.

M: Yeah, it didn't matter. And when you were in your car, you were just in your car; you weren't going to get a phone call. There was no reason to be crashing your car because you desperately needed to text somebody. Because you're in your car, it's your private time, you're alone. And at home, the same thing. I loved that. I drive down Harper all the time. Every time I'm in that neighborhood, I drive down Harper and I slow down in front of that building because I loved living there.

N: It was a great home.

M: And it was a simple life, and in many ways richer because we had time for things like, oh, I don't know, a social life. Going out to dinner. Just hanging out and doing nothing. Can you imagine? *(Laughs)*
But ultimately, you just have to do the things that you love to do. Sometimes I get overwhelmed by the fact that Nick and I get to do so many of those things professionally. If our goal is to work on good material with nice people who are good at their jobs, the amount of times we get to do that, with all three of those boxes being ticked off, is pretty incredible. Sometimes only one or two of the boxes are ticked off, and then it's maybe not as great. Or none of the boxes. But that's the life of a betting man.

N: That's the exception, not the rule.

M: Clearly, you haven't yet done an I Can't Believe It's Not Butter commercial.

Also, I just want to say that no one should be discouraged from trying their hand at any discipline that they're attracted to. You have the freedom to do it. Whether you're going to be amazing at it remains to be seen. But you should be able to try yourself out, and it's nice to have a lot of little fun things at hand to take your mind off of all the stresses of daily life.

N: It is.

M: Anything you can lose yourself in, do it. Whether it's going on a hike, or drawing a picture, or calling your best friend on the phone, do that. I guess I'm done.

N: The end.

M: I have a new topic.

N: The topic is . . .

M: Dogs!

N: Dogs.

M: We have good dogs. We've always had good dogs.

N: Yeah, we met partly over Willa, who was our first dog that Megan rescued a few months before . . .

M: Before I rescued you.

N: Before you rescued me. And we were both bedraggled, in need of nutrition.

M: Both wearing golden overalls. It was very strange.

N: Wasn't there something to it? When you brought Willa to rehearsal, I was good with her?

M: Yes, I had to bring Willa with me a few times to rehearsal because I lived by myself. Nick was the only one who really played with her, which I thought was very sweet. Little did I know he was trying to get into my pannies.

N: It wasn't the only play I was making. . . . I love dogs. If somebody's got an animal around, I want to be friends with it.

M: We spend a lot of time talking about our dog Clover because she's a magical creature. It's like having a fairy that's lying curled up in the bed with you.

N: For over five years she has astonished us daily with her personality.

M: He came up earlier and said, "Can you make Clover stop making me laugh so much?" I said, "I don't know. I don't think that's possible."

N: You already had Willa when we met so it was kind of in place, but I feel like the presence of dogs in our lives has allowed us to not feel like two lonely old clowns living in the hills.

M: Yeah. I never think of them as, like, children substitutes or something, but I do think it's really nice to have these little beings that grace us with their presence.

N: Willa, our first dog, was amazing. She seemed like she had some sort of holy powers, or like she was channeling a being of great wisdom. I always said she really ran the house, and we got Elmo a couple of years later as a companion to Willa. He was kind of a good-time Charlie, just always happy to be the lieutenant and down with whatever the rest of us were up to. But I feel like Clover has now taken the best of those qualities and become an even greater household leader.

M: Yes, we've had all great dogs. Clover is a little dog who loves everybody and doesn't bark and she loves to play. She's a really easy dog to travel with and she's so fun to be around. She brings us a lot of joy. All of our dogs have brought us so much joy.

N: Clover is also talented and game to get onstage. We incorporated her into our touring comedy show.

M: Yeah, she's completely unflappable. Bring her out onstage in a theater with two thousand people and she's just unfazed. She'll go right down to the lip of the stage with her tail wagging and try to meet people in the front row. She's unbothered by applause or laughter or anything like that. She likes treats, though.

N: She does like a treat.

M: But I think we've taught our dogs, been consistent in training them, for whatever that's worth, so we've had good luck with them not having annoying habits like begging for food. Or humping people. Or ...

N: Or barking. That's what people comment on the most: "Your dog is so cool."

M: Plot twist! So we were not discussing getting another dog, and I was not thinking about it. Then last Tuesday, I was driving down the street, and I saw a sign that said "Dog Adoptions." I thought, "I'd better go in there." And now we have Buddy.

N: *(As Megan)* "That was nice of them to put out a sign for me. How'd they know I was going to be driving this way?"

M: We got the cutest, sweetest little dog in the world. He's like a male version of Clover. Why is it so great to bring a new little dog home? It's maybe like those people I've heard about who have these things called "children" that bring you love and joy. It might be akin to that, in a certain way.

N: I don't understand why people don't train their kids to poop in the yard, though. Everyone gripes about the diapers. And I think, "We don't need no diapers."
But this is a good example of how we deal: I was in a meeting at my shop on the east side of LA. And Megan starts texting me pictures of a strange, cute dog. And I just thought, "Oh, shit." After the third picture, I texted back, "What's going on?" and she texted, "Do you think you could come over to this dog adoption

place? They close at seven." And I said, "I don't think I can—this meeting goes until 6:30."

M: And he was leaving town the next morning. At, like, six in the morning.

N: And I think to myself, "What the fuck are you doing?" I'm leaving at six in the morning for a bunch of work away from home, and you know, there was a level of annoyance to it. I have to go home and pack, it's the end of my day . . .

M: I knew he was going to come, though.

N: There were a couple of babies at the meeting. A couple of the shop bosses are ladies with new babies. And the babies were griping. So the meeting ended at six, a little early. So I texted Megan and said that I could make it over there.

M: I knew he was going to come.

N: So I did. And we met Buddy, and he's fantastic.

M: He's our buddy!

N: I was just glad that I didn't do a grumpy Fred Flintstone and say, "Fucking go home! What are you doing at a dog adoption place!" But instead . . .

M: Part of that might also be predicated on the fact that as irritating as it might have been in the moment, and also out of the blue because we weren't talking about getting a dog, I think it could be said that you're aware that I'm an excellent dog-picker-outer.

N: That is without question. But it had more to do with taking a deep breath and being Zen about it. It wasn't, "This is going to be a good dog." It was, "If your gut took you into that place . . ."

M: Well, I was on my way somewhere else. I wasn't planning to look for a dog. And I saw this building that said "Dog Adoptions." And I thought, "I have to go in there." I didn't even go to the other place, I went to "Dog Adoptions." They didn't really even have that many dogs, and I thought, "I'm not going to find a dog where there's, like, five dogs." And then there's this perfect dog.

N: For me, the lesson is—and the older I get, the more I learn this lesson—I literally think, "If I say no right now, it will create negativity. It will create badness."

M: You could have said no, but then you wouldn't have met Buddy.

N: Right. But if I say yes, the worst thing that happens is that I spend an extra thirty minutes looking at dogs in West Hollywood. But if you say yes, you keep yourself open to a chance that a great new B/buddy will come into your life.

M: So he got there, and our assistant had brought Clover over to make sure she would approve of this new dog, because ultimately she has the final say. *(Laughs)* And they seemed to hit it off as well as dogs will upon first meeting. And about five minutes in, I said to Nick, "What do you think?" And he said, "I love him." And I said, "I knew you would!" He's our buddy.

I do think that having our dogs—we're saps in that regard—is a big part of our life. And dogs are funky fresh.

N: More to the point, it's occurring to me that what we do for a living is keep it fresh. We're so lucky that we can— we love to read, consume, and perform in so many different ways. And so we're able to look at the different outlets in our lives on every given day and say, "Today I'm just going to read this great book." Then we might say, "I'm going to call up my agent and option this book." Or I'll call my agent and see who's doing a play I just read. The fact that we're able to find things we're passionate about and to create works of art that can bring people some laughter or good feelings is a very lucky vocation.

M: But on the other side of it, for us, keeping it fresh is sort of the opposite of what other people might think. Other people might think, "I'm going to keep it fresh by wearing a trench coat with nothing underneath, and then I'm going to drop it to the floor when he walks in the front door!" We don't do that kind of stuff. Our version of keeping it fresh would be boring, because we like to watch movies and television, we like to listen to books while we do puzzles, or we read actual physical books and then trade, or we play with the dogs—it's not a whirlwind of excitement at our house. But that's when we're happiest, and that's when we're at our best. When we have time to do those introverty things that we like to do. When we can be introverts together.

N: Because of our voracious professional lives, the novel choice is to not work. What if we don't look at emails? What if we don't attend to our seventeen responsibilities? What if we do a fucking puzzle? That shit is fresh.

M: That's it. You said it, brother. This book is sponsored by the International Puzzles Society. (Ad)

N: Is that it?

M: That's the end of the book.

N: The end. Bye.

M: Best book ever!

N: Naa-na-na-na-naa. Fart!

M: Classic.

Acknowledgments

THE AUTHORS WOULD LIKE TO THANK EACH OTHER FOR their immeasurable support and tough love throughout this process. They would also like to thank their redoubtable editor, Jill Something; their winsome agents, Monika Verma and Daniel Greenberg; and their trusty assistants, Michael Landry and Emily Bernstein. Finally, of course none of this could have been pulled off, literally or figuratively, without the stalwart crew at Dutton: Christine Ball, John Parsley, Carrie Swetonic, Elina Vaysbeyn, Amanda Walker, Jamie Knapp, Emily Canders, Marya Pasciuto, LeeAnn Pemberton, Cassandra Garruzzo, and Dora Mak.

Credits

Book Design: Megan Mullally
Photography: Emily Shur
Illustrations: Meryl Rowin
Layouts: Cassandra Garruzzo
Stylist: Shirley Kurata
Hair: John Ruggiero
Makeup: Sandy Ganzer
Set Design: Kendall and Meagan Faeth
Puzzle Photos: Marcus Stuckey and Michael Landry

About The Authors

NICK OFFERMAN AND MEGAN MULLALLY ARE ACTORS, PER-
formers, and comedians. Together they have appeared in the
television shows *Will & Grace*, *Parks & Recreation*, and
Childrens Hospital; the movies *Somebody Up There Likes
Me*, *The Kings of Summer*, *Infinity Baby*, and *Smashed*; and the
comedy tour *Summer of 69: No Apostrophe*. They live in Los
Angeles, California, with their poodles.